Along with *Guidelines* this ye[...]
At first I wondered how I wou[...]
devotions but it is proving a w[...]
to limit how much I read in on[...]
read within a couple of weeks [...]
be still before God and meditate on his word. It will now be a
regular order.

HOWARD HUTCHINGS

I really like the simple practical and creative suggestions of ways
to make prayer come alive—for example, encouragements to go
out into the garden and see prayer as living, not just reciting
words.

APRIL MCINTYRE

There seems to be something for everyone and I look forward to
what each section has to offer.

MARY TAYLOR

I have found the meditations very helpful and have used them in
a small group setting, which has been so useful in helping others
to achieve that place of stillness and connection with the living
God. For me it works that I don't have to do one section every
day, just within the two weeks. Thank you all for helping me on
my journey.

ROSY RUSSELL

Quiet Spaces offers a welcome and imaginative complement to
traditional daily Bible notes, with scriptural and other Christian
themes to ponder and pray with over periods of two weeks. The
flexible format is most helpful, as we can use the reflections in
whatever way fits best in our particular lifestyle.

ANGELA ASHWIN

Contents

Text copyright © BRF 2016
Authors retain copyright in their own work

Published by
The Bible Reading Fellowship
15 The Chambers
Abingdon, OX14 3FE
United Kingdom
Tel: +44 (0)1865 319700
Email: enquiries@brf.org.uk
Website: www.brf.org.uk
BRF is a Registered Charity

ISBN 978 0 85746 403 3
First published 2016
10 9 8 7 6 5 4 3 2 1 0

Acknowledgements
Scripture quotations taken from The Holy Bible, Today's New International Version,
copyright © 2004 by Biblica. Used by permission of Hodder & Stoughton Publishers, a
Hachette UK company. All rights reserved. 'TNIV' is a registered trademark of Biblica.

Scripture quotations taken from The Holy Bible, New International Version (Anglicised
edition) copyright © 1973, 1978, 1984, 2011 by Biblica. Used by permission of Hodder &
Stoughton Publishers, an Hachette UK company. All rights reserved. 'NIV' is a registered
trade mark of Biblica (formerly International Bible Society). UK trademark number
1448790.

Scripture quotations taken from The New Revised Standard Version of the Bible, Anglicised
Edition, copyright © 1989, 1995 by the Division of Christian Education of the National
Council of the Churches of Christ in the USA, and are used by permission. All rights
reserved.

Scripture quotations from THE MESSAGE. Copyright © by Eugene H. Peterson 1993, 1994,
1995. Used by permission of NavPress Publishing Group.

Extract from As a Child by Phil Steer, published by lulu.com, 2012

Cover photograph: © Thinkstock

Every effort has been made to trace and contact copyright owners for material used in
this resource. We apologise for any inadvertent omissions or errors, and would ask those
concerned to contact us so that full acknowledgement can be made in the future.

A catalogue record for this book is available from the British Library

Printed by Gutenberg Press, Tarxien, Malta

The Editor writes...

Welcome to this issue of *Quiet Spaces*.

This issue covers a lovely range of seasons, with the fantastic colours of autumn, the cold of winter, brightened up by the sparkle and colour of Christmas. Despite the weather, it is a season for getting out, especially in the early weeks when the leaves are falling from the trees and giving us such a multi-coloured reminder of God's presence. For me it is a time when the house fills with things I've picked up on a walk: the red and orange leaves that speak of God's generosity, the acorns, conkers and other seeds that remind me of the continuing cycle of life which will bring new birth and new stages of life, and the last few flowers, reminding me that God's creativity does not take a break over the winter. After the warmth of summer, the cold mornings of autumn come as a surprise, but we can enjoy the freshness they bring, and experience the revelation that occurs as the early morning mist lifts and we can see the world again.

So maybe this autumn you could try and get out more, see the wonder of God's creation first hand. It doesn't have to be a long walk, but spend time looking and watching and seeing what you usually miss as you rush by.

And the things you bring home: don't just leave them on the hall table; try looking more closely at them. Get to know them and then allow them to speak to you. Share them with their creator God, who loves them. He also loves you enough to send his son, Jesus, to be born as a vulnerable baby. Try starting to prepare for Christmas early by pausing and looking for God in the unexpected places—by Christmas you'll be an expert!

I pray that this issue of *Quiet Spaces* will help you as you pause and seek God; that you will be able to find the time and space to be quiet and to be with God. And remember, we always like to hear how you get on in your journey into *Quiet Spaces*.

Sally Smith

Writers in this issue

Jean Watson is a writer, editor, spiritual director and trustee of a local counselling service. Her work has included teaching, writing and editing for children and adults, and her articles, stories and scripts have been published in books and magazines and used on radio and TV.

Sister Jean Marie Dwyer is a Dominican Nun of the Queen of Peace Monastery, Squamish, British Columbia, Canada. The monastery is dedicated to silence, prayer, study and intercession for all people. She is the author of *The Sacred Place of Prayer* (BRF, 2013) and *The Unfolding Journey: the God Within: Etty Hillesum and Meister Eckhart* (Novalis, 2014).

Sally Smith enjoys creating spaces that enable encounters with God through leading Quiet Days and creating prayer corners and stations. She has led prayer groups in her local church, works as a spiritual director and writes and produces education materials.

Liz Hoare is tutor in spiritual formation at Wycliffe Hall in Oxford. She teaches discipleship and prayer and has a special interest in spiritual direction. She is married to Toddy, a sculptor, and they have a son. Liz enjoys baking, the English countryside and looking after her chickens.

Anne Noble grew up on Merseyside and studied geology at Oxford and Toronto. She is a Team Vicar in Nottingham and is married with two grown-up daughters. She still enjoys geology, reflecting on what we can hear and see of the God of all time through rocks. In her spare time she loves gardening.

Sally Welch is Vicar of Charlbury with Shorthampton and Area Dean of Chipping Norton in the Diocese of Oxford. She is a writer and lecturer on spirituality, and is particularly interested in pilgrimage and labyrinth. She has made many pilgrimages both in England and Europe.

Susan Blagden is training officer for Bangor Diocese (Church in Wales) and an Oblate of the Community of St Mary the Virgin. She is also the founder of Contemplative Camera, exploring the relationship between contemplative prayer and photography—see www.contemplativecamera.org.

Helen Julian CSF is an Anglican Franciscan sister, currently serving her community as Minister General. She also has a ministry as a priest, has written three books for BRF and contributes to BRF's Bible reading notes *New Daylight*.

What story am I in?

Jean Watson

My story

Introduction

We all have a life story and within it are smaller stories or aspects of the main story. But have you ever had the chance to reflect deeply on it all? I have—and it was one of the most transformative experiences of my life.

I invite you to think about your whole life story or your smaller faith story by first identifying some of the significant small stories—about people, events, experiences—within it, and gradually to build up a kind of collage of them. To do this you will need a large sheet of paper, some Post-it notes, writing and drawing materials, glue or sticky tape and assorted objects you'll collect along the way. Using the Post-it notes you'll be able to move them round as your story unfolds and as patterns or journeys develop. You can look at your life story or your faith story, or, more likely, the interweaving of the two.

Read Psalm 23. This could be said to be David's story in brief. In lives as in stories, the characters involved are important. Who does David regard as the main character in his life/faith story in this psalm? This is how he writes about the main character: 'The Lord is my shepherd.'

If you were writing a psalm about your story how might you finish the sentence beginning: 'The Lord is my...'? You might like to write this completed sentence on one of your Post-it notes and put it somewhere on your large sheet of paper.

Spiritual refreshment

Creative

Read Psalm 23, looking for the places where David is refreshed or rested. What does he receive from God that restores him and enables him to carry on?

Has a time of spiritual refreshment occurred in your story? Hopefully, there have been many such times. Where, when and how were you, or are you, spiritually refreshed? You might have been refreshed, for example, through a quiet day, a particular person, place, book, holiday, course of study...

Draw or find pictures or photos that symbolise your 'green pastures' and 'quiet waters' experiences. Spend time with your pictures, receiving that peace and rest again from God.

Use some oil to anoint yourself afresh (on your hands or forehead) and add a drop of oil to one of your Post-it notes (see Psalm 23:5).

You might like to take another of your Post-it notes and write about whatever or whoever refreshed you.

For this time of refreshment in my life—thank you, my Good Shepherd.
Lord, I need and ask you for a time of refreshment in my life right now...

Parables from creation

Going out

In any story the setting is important. The author takes time to describe where the action is taking place. Similarly our surroundings—nature, creation—play a part in all our stories. I invite you to think about the part surroundings have played or are now playing in yours.

Read Psalm 104:24.

Does the following quotation ring any bells for you?

'As we wait on a God we don't fully know and will never fully understand, the natural world conveys something of the mystery and wonder of God that might just provoke the inspiration to be amazed.' It comes from a book by Graham B. Usher (*Places of Enchantment, Meeting God in landscapes*, SPCK, 2012, p. xiv). The author looks at various aspects of landscape—forest, river, mountain, desert, sky—and shows that scripturally and in people's lives they are important and inspirational.

If you possibly can, spend time in a garden or outdoors somewhere taking in the sights, sounds, smells, life and activity all around you. What impact do the surroundings have on your body, mind, emotions or spirit? Does the world about you tell you anything about God's character or ways? Spend time allowing God to use the setting to speak to you. You may find you focus on a flower or tree or view that sums up some part of your life.

You may want to take a leaf or something back with you to add to your life collage, or you could write or draw about any significant outdoor places that have meant a lot in your story on a Post-it note and put it on your collage.

Reflecting on this poem could prompt you to pray or praise.

> *Earth's crammed with heaven,*
> *And every common bush afire with God;*
> *But only he who sees, takes off his shoes,*
> *The rest sit round it and pick blackberries.*

ELIZABETH BARRETT BROWNING (1806–61)

Conversion or transformation

Creative

Stories often have some conversion or transformation event in them. Read Acts 26:12–23 and look for signs of conversion or transformation.

A light and voice from heaven: Paul's conversion story was very dramatic and unusual. Perhaps yours is utterly different or you may have had several points in your story when, dramatically or very quietly, new light, new truth, had a transforming effect or showed you the way forward.

If you have a small piece of tarnished silver, a tiny spoon perhaps, you could polish it and transform it into sparkling silver, or leave a copper coin in vinegar or ketchup for a while then see how it has been transformed and reflect on your own transformation. Stick your shining objects on your collage.

Write or draw about your conversion on transformation story on a Post-it note and arrange it and the other notes on your large sheet of paper.

Lord, thank you for the images of transformation in scripture— for your promises to wash us whiter than snow, to refine us like gold and silver. Help me to be open to being changed and transformed as I journey with you.

Choices and consequences

Creative

In every story there are moments when a character has to make a choice. How the story develops will depend on what they choose at this point.

All our stories are full of choices and their consequences. Spend a few moments thinking about some of yours.

The stories of Judas and Peter illustrate very starkly the difference between making a bad choice which depresses and ultimately destroys a person and one that humbles and changes him or her for the better.

Read Matthew 26:25, 75.

Judas betrayed Jesus to the Jewish authorities and this was one of the factors that brought about the crucifixion. He realised that he had sinned and gave back the money he had received for the information he had given, but then, remorseful and guilty, went and hanged himself.

Peter had also betrayed Jesus by denying that he even knew him, but his reaction was to go out and weep bitterly; and when Jesus later reproved him—no, he didn't!—he gently but persistently asked him whether he loved him, Peter, repentant and emotionally very affected, I am sure—macho man though he appeared to be—replied that he did (John 21:15–17).

I have always been struck by the contrast between Peter and Judas in the choices they made at these key moments in their lives.

Your choices and their consequences may not be as dramatic as either Judas' or Peter's. Did you, perhaps, decide to move, change jobs, marry, have children, take a risk of some sort?

You could draw or make a signpost out of drinking straws or twigs, with arms pointing in opposite directions to symbolise your experience. As you work, allow God to show the ways you have followed, or not, his directing and the directions he is asking you to take in the future. Add your signpost to your collage.

On a Post-it note write or draw about choices and consequences that were most significant in your story and arrange or re-arrange it and the other notes on your large sheet of paper.

Thank you for the signpost of the cross. I want to listen to what you want to say to me as I contemplate its message...

Overcoming monsters or giants

Creative

Stories contain subplots that challenge the characters. There may be times when they are in a dark and difficult place or come up against something that feels overwhelming.

David, the shepherd, king and psalmist, had many such experiences. Read about one of them in 1 Samuel 17:45–50.

A newspaper headline—had there been one—might have read:

> ## Little and Large
> Young, inexperienced Israelite shepherd boy David encounters massive Philistine champion Goliath...

What helped you when you faced your 'monster' or were stuck in your 'dark place'?

Write about it. As you think about this you could draw a hand or draw round your hand to symbolise a helping hand. Remember how Help in *The Pilgrim's Progress* stretched out his hand to pull Christian out of his Slough of Despond? Add your hand and writing to your collage.

Lord, I reflect thankfully on all the forms of help that I have received when I needed it...

Here is some good news

Reflective

In the best stories the main characters will have both good and
bad experiences. As you think about your story, with all its ups
and downs, do you see it mainly in a positive or negative light?

Read Luke 2:10.

The gospel is meant to be good news, to turn our lives,
basically and ultimately, into good news stories. Can you
identify with this as you look at your story?

The broadcast/televised news is often dreadful. One of the
reasons I enjoy listening to 'Saturday Live' on Radio 4 is that
it is full of laughter and good news including stories of people
who want to identify, make contact with and thank others for
kindness shown to them at difficult times.

Sometimes the gospel is presented as rather bad news: do this,
tick these boxes or else... Jesus came to set us free from sin and
free to live life well and fully. Of course, this involves honestly
facing our frailties and failures and a willingness to grow and
change—but with the help of the one who is love and only
wants what's best for us.

A distorted picture of God can hold us back in our relationship
with him.

'Our story is written by God who is more than author, he is the
romantic lead in our personal drama. He created us for himself
and now he is moving heaven and earth to restore us to his
side... We are not pond scum, nor are we the lead in the story.
We are the Beloved' (*The Sacred Romance,* Curtis & Eldredge,
Thomas Nelson, 1997, pp.147, 148).

'As Luther discovered, through Jesus we may know that God
is a Father and "we may look into his fatherly heart and sense
how boundlessly he loves us"' (*The Good God*, Michael Reeves,

Paternoster, 2012, p. 107). Is your relationship with God as warm and reassuring as that suggested in these quotes? You may want to thank God for this or talk to him about anything that troubles you as a result of your reflections.

Take a Post-it note and write or draw what your *feelings* tell you about your life story right now—whether it feels like a good, bad or difficult news story—and then, if it's different, what your *faith* tells you about the overall direction of your life story.

Or you could cut out words or phrases from newspapers to make a good-news headline that rings true for you and for your life and faith.

Bring to God your faith and your feelings—of trust, thankfulness, pain, bewilderment...

The search for love

Creative

The search for something is a common theme within stories and within people's lives. It might be a search for fame, power or money. But even more compelling for most us, I suggest, is the search for love—particularly for one enduring love.

But what is love? A 'many-splendoured thing', for sure. In C.S. Lewis' book *The Four Loves* he identifies romantic love (*eros*), friendship (*philia*), affection (*storge*) and unconditional (*divine*) love (*agape*).

Which kinds of love do you think the following Bible verses perhaps indicate?

'A friend loves at all times' (Proverbs 17:17, TNIV).

'The disciple whom Jesus loved was reclining next to him' (John 13:23).

'Keep on loving one another as brothers and sisters' (Hebrews 13:1).

'Love one another deeply, from the heart' (1 Peter 1:22).
'I have loved you with an everlasting love' (Jeremiah 31:3).
'My beloved is mine and I am his' (Song of Songs 2:16).

What has been your experience of love in any of its splendours? I was blessed enough to want one enduring intimate love and to have it until my husband's sudden and unexpected death after 32 years of marriage. But some of the people I meet have also longed for that experience but have not found it. We all need to experience different forms of love.

On your next Post-it note, write or draw about your experience of love (human or divine or both) and its impact on your story.

You could draw or find and cut out a picture that symbolises the mutual cherishing that love at its best offers and receives. Use it to receive that love from God.

You may want to spend time re-arranging your Post-it notes, drawings and objects in relation to one another.

Lord, I am a learner in your school of love. Please teach me and help me to be teachable.

Right about turn

Creative

There is often a turning point in a story when the whole direction changes suddenly.

I wonder whether your life story has had some 'turn around' points—points at which you have made a radical change for the better in yourself, in your circumstances, in the direction in which you were going. Part of the good news for followers of Jesus is that at any point, our lives can be turned around. Many life-stories bear testimony to this as do many stories in the Bible, including the story of the thief on the cross and the prodigal son. Ruth Etchells wrote the poem 'Ballad of the Judas Tree' about Judas after his apparent final end, in which she imagines Jesus rescuing Judas from hell (see 1 Peter 3:18–20). Search online for the poem or find it in *The Journey* by John Pritchard, SPCK, 2014 (pp. 103, 104).

We should not limit Christ's power and love; and, however badly we are spiralling down, we can be 'ransomed, healed, restored, forgiven' and start or return to walking on 'the king's highway', as John Bunyan put it in *The Pilgrim's Progress*.

Read Luke 15:11–24. As you read, list the significant words in the son's downward spiral, and those that describe his right about turn.

Your right about turns may not have been as dramatic as the one in our Bible story; perhaps there have been smaller wrong turnings or compromises and less dramatic changes for the better here and there. Draw a U-turn or fashion one out of plasticine or Blu-Tack® and, as you do so, invite God into your U-turns. Then place it on your paper to symbolise your right-about-turn experience.

On another Post-it note, write about or draw a significant right about turn in the past or one that you are facing at the moment. Reflect in God's presence on the turning points in your life and faith.

Thorns and other problems

Creative

In all our life and faith stories in this world we encounter problems and difficulties. The apostle Paul called a seemingly intractable problem he faced—no one knows for sure what it was—a 'thorn'.

Read 2 Corinthians 12:7b–10. Note especially: 'My grace is sufficient for you, for my power is made perfect in weakness' (2 Corinthians 12:9 TNIV).

Paul regarded his 'thorn' as sent by God to teach him a lesson. Many of us, myself included, prefer to make a distinction between what God directly *sends* and what he *allows* through which, with his help and that of his human 'agents' and 'angels', we can learn and grow and then be a help to others.

I wrote these notes as I was doing very well after a hip operation. And then I fell heavily on the pavement and once again I was hobbling painfully on two sticks. This was a 'thorn' for me—thankfully not a permanent one. Are there 'thorns' with which you live or which have come your way from time to time? What is your experience of praying about these? Draw or find a thorn to symbolise a particularly difficult time in your story. Allow its sharpness to remind you of where God was in the pain.

Write about or draw one of your experiences of encountering a difficulty and the outcome.

Talk to God about your experience of how his grace is sufficient for you, or pray that you will experience his sufficient grace in whatever way it comes.

Helpers and friends

Creative

We were made for relationships—that is possibly the most important 'r' in our life and faith stories. Who are the people who have been important in your life/faith story?

In sermons and hymns I have often heard or seen the sound-bite: 'All you need is Jesus.' But is that true in experience? Yes, we need Jesus as our Saviour and friend who makes God

17

accessible to us and us to God. But Jesus, who lived in close dependence on the Father and the Spirit, also needed his apostles and other people to be with him, to listen to him and help him; and Paul needed his fellow-labourers. Talking about God's ways and means of helping us—speaking to us, caring and providing for us, encouraging us—focuses on his creativity and his graciousness.

Read 1 Corinthians 12:7, 13, 20–27.

We are 'the body of Christ'—in other words Christ is the head of the body which is 'put... together' by God and 'baptised by one Spirit'. The phrase that stands out for me is the one about God wanting the parts of the body to have 'equal concern for each other'. But from the first verse in our passage which speaks about the manifestation of the Spirit being given 'for the common good' and from other parts of the Bible, I believe our concern for others should not end with fellow-believers; we live within a global as well as a Christian community, from both of which we receive much and to both of which we therefore have a responsibility to contribute much.

Draw or find a picture or a photograph that symbolises fellowship or friendship for you.

On a Post-it note, write about some significant help or helpers you have benefited from in your life/faith story and put it where appropriate on your large sheet of paper.

Lord, I want to thank you particularly for... (Question to self: 'Have I thanked them—or at least shown my gratitude to them—as well?')

Living in two stories

Creative

As followers of Jesus we have to try to balance the act of living in two stories—our present earthly story and our present and future heavenly story. It's not easy to avoid being so heavenly minded that we're no earthly use or vice versa! Perhaps today's verses are helpful here.

'In the beginning God created the heavens and the earth' (Genesis 1:1, TNIV).

'Heaven is my throne, and the earth is my footstool' (Isaiah 66:1).

'The earth will be filled with the knowledge of the Lord as the waters cover the sea' (Isaiah 11:9).

'The earth is full of his unfailing love' (Psalm 33:5).

'The eyes of the Lord range throughout the earth to strengthen those whose hearts are fully committed to him' (2 Chronicles 16:9).

'Your kingdom come, your will be done on earth as it is in heaven' (Matthew 6:10).

'The kingdom of the world has become the kingdom of our Lord and of his Messiah, and he will reign for ever and ever' (Revelation 11:15).

As you read, look for the ways in which God created, is at work in and cares for the earth, the world, the cosmos. By implication so should we, because he has planned that one day all will be one with heaven—restored and renewed and under the reign and rule of God for ever.

Cut a circle out of kitchen foil and a smaller one out of tracing paper and place the smaller circle in the centre of the bigger one, to symbolise two worlds or stories, with one—the heavenly world or story—surrounding and shining through to the other: our earthly world or story. Write about or draw your experience of trying to live in two stories.

You might also like to take your large piece of paper and write in the middle of it: *Who and where I am now*; then rearrange your other Post-it notes, drawings, objects and so on around it, thinking about how the person you are now has been and is being affected by the different people, events and experiences within your life/faith story. You might also like to add additional words to your sentence beginning: The Lord is my... ; these could be other descriptions or names of God which your life/faith story in any of its aspects prompts you to do. To put it another way, over the years what has this main character in your story, and in your small stories within that, come to mean for you?

God, help me to make the most of and give the most to each present moment and to use some of those present moments to dwell on, bask in and be warmed and encouraged by thoughts of my past and my unimaginably wonderful eternal future—all of which have been 'sorted' by your grace and love.

Finding and living in the 'now' of God

Jean Marie Dwyer OP

The eternal now

Introduction

We live in a society that is constantly on the go. We have lost sight of what it means to be reflective. Our busy world does not give us the chance to stop or to think and this can dull our search for happiness and truth. Learning to live in the present moment makes it possible to counteract this tendency in modern life. In this section we will explore an understanding of what it means to live in the present moment, a constant theme found in spiritual writings and in the lives of men and women who enter into deep relationship with God.

The present moment is the only point of time we can work with. Only in the present moment do we encounter God. The Dominican mystic Meister Eckhart calls it the 'now' of God and relates it to the presence of the eternal in time: it is the place of encounter with God.

In the following sections I want to offer some practical suggestions for how we can reclaim the 'eternal now' in our lives. Doing so is not complicated or beyond us. We simply need to live fully aware of today, savouring it, touching with awareness the events and circumstances of each day, using our senses with mindfulness—and above all living the movements of the day with heightened attentiveness and presence to reality.

As human beings we exist both bodily and spiritually. So we need to be present to our body as well as becoming more aware of the inner reality of our spirit. We will begin with the practice of heightened awareness, of standing within our body, being present to our self, to others and to the world about us. Starting with the bodily practice will give us a good place from which to then proceed to an awareness of the spiritual dynamic of living in the present moment, searching for the way to find the 'now' of God.

Mindfulness

Prayer

All that we look at, our presence to things, events or people, or our presence to our deepest centre or God is about *mindfulness*, being aware and mindful of what is within and without. So often we go through our day without really being mindful, without really noticing. We let events move us along without any reflection. We are not consciously present to what comes into our day and often do not really see the people we encounter. In order to be in the present moment we need to be mindful—touch, taste and see the reality that each moment brings. We cultivate a living and active relationship with God by cultivating mindfulness.

Lord, open my eyes that I may see—heal my blindness. I want to see with new eyes your creation, my brothers and sisters in their unique giftedness, the circumstances of my life from your perspective. Draw me into the light of your Holy Spirit that everything that comes into my day may be filled with the radiance of your glory. Help me to be mindful of your presence with me in each moment. Amen

Be where you are

Creative

Our modern culture has lost the ability to be where they are, to exist in the moment, present to others and to the environment. Just watch people at an airport. They are plugged in listening to music, watching their computers preparing for the next important meeting or presentation, oblivious to what or who is around them. It is common to see people walking with someone and talking to someone else on their mobile phone. These are typical examples of not being present to the moment. What do you do that stops you being mindful of where you are?

An exercise of being present:

1. You may want to take your shoes off for this exercise. Stand in your room and close your eyes, be aware of your feet, feel them planted firmly on the floor—take several minutes just to sense your feet and the fact of your being grounded in a place.

2. Open your eyes and look around at the pictures, the furniture and the objects in your room. Walk around touching things; focus on one item at a time: touching it, looking at its colour, its newness or oldness. See this very familiar space with new eyes, conscious of the multi-layered meanings it has for you. Be attentive to the room, this moment and nothing else. Don't be in a hurry.

3. Continue this practice throughout a day. When you wake in the morning look around and be attentive to the new day. Can you feel its newness enter into you? Be open to surprises—be delicately perceptive to your world.

4. Practise this awareness in other spaces you are in during the day. It can develop into an inner consciousness of being present to the place and to the people you meet—being attentive in a new way.

Wasting time

Reflective

We live in a very pragmatic world where everything is judged by productivity. Wasting time is not on our agenda. I use the word 'wasting' to help us recognise that we do not always have to be achievers. We can relax and let go; actually it is essential to our wholeness that we do so. A world of achievers encourages an unhealthy competitive spirit and one-upmanship. This can result in a real tendency to be driven, which militates against our ability to be still and be present.

It is important that we examine our attitudes and the way in which we live our life. St Paul's teaching on the use of our gifts for the common good is the Christian spirit rather than driven competitiveness.

'The gifts he gave were that some would be apostles, some prophets, some evangelists, some pastors and teachers, to equip the saints for the work of ministry, for building up the body of Christ, until all of us come to the unity of the faith and of the knowledge of the Son of God, to maturity, to the measure of the full stature of Christ' (Ephesians 4:11–13, NRSV).

Even our leisure time can be filled with activity and doing— granted fun times, exercise, sports, are important, but we need to add one more necessary dimension of leisure directly related to human well-being, that of reflection and contemplation. For the early Greek philosophers the highest meaning of leisure was contemplation. How many of us would equate time off and relaxation with reflection?

Aristotle believed that the human person's highest activity was reason—our ability to be aware. He says we are meant to be thinking, reflective creatures and the highest attainment of our nature is to be contemplative. One of the key words related to human happiness is being contemplative. We need leisure to be contemplative, to be human and to be happy. In the *Nicomachean Ethics* Aristotle writes 'we are busy that we may have leisure'. Do you ever consider that you are busy in order to have time for leisure, a rather shocking statement and completely counter-cultural for us?

- Reflect on the thought 'that we are busy so that we may have leisure'. Do you agree? What meaning do you find in it? Is it helpful?
- Pray over the phrase, holding it as you come before God. Record your thoughts in your journal.

Or you could take a chair into your garden. Put your feet up and just sit there doing nothing, not even planning all the things you need to get done or want to accomplish. Keep emptying your mind of thoughts and just be there doing nothing. For many of us it will be hard work. Try to do this for at least 20 minutes. Form a habit of doing this two or three times a week until you can be comfortable with just being. It is a good ongoing practice to cultivate until a habit is formed within you.

An exercise of focusing

Going out

As you practise focusing on reality, you might like to try the following examples. You are developing your mindfulness of the people and things around you, and of your own body. Become more aware of the reality around you.

Many people eat on the run and do not take time to be really present and thankful for the food they eat. Sit down to a home-cooked meal (not fast food). Be aware of the colour, arrangement and taste of the food. Eat very slowly—chew everything at least ten times. This helps us to become conscious of ordinary daily events in our life. The practice really slows us down in order to raise our consciousness to the present act.

To explore presence to nature, try taking a solitary walk and then find a small rock and sit down where you can see it. Contemplate the rock for 15 minutes—its feel, its shape, its beauty and interesting facets—just gaze at that rock, until it becomes a part of your understanding.

How do you feel? Have you found beauty? How has this simple exercise in silent attentiveness affected you? How has it enabled you to become aware of reality in a new way? How can you use this knowledge to change your life?

Inattentiveness

Reflection

I have outlined various ways of attentively being present to reality as a preparation for living in the present moment. Let us now think about what causes us to be inattentive. It is our sin and brokenness. Our culture has been desensitised to sin. It denies the existence of sin even in the face of the experience of brokenness and dysfunction. Because of this our society lives in a state of forgetfulness of where our true centre resides. Christians reverse this forgetfulness by remembering. Each one of us needs to be present consciously and dynamically to our rootedness in God.

Focus on your inner spirit.

Reflect on the teaching of this section.

Do I agree? In your journal rewrite the teaching in your own words.

How do you need to transform your thoughts?

What is within you that needs change?

Have a plan for living more dynamically and focused on God.

Attunement: contemplative awareness

Visual/creative

'Now the word of the Lord came to me saying, "Before I formed you in the womb I knew you, and before you were born I consecrated you; I appointed you a prophet to the nations"' (Jeremiah 1:4–5, NRSV).

God is always present to us. He knows us, sustains us and loves us with an infinite love at every moment. If that was not true we would cease to exist. God desires us to come to an awareness of his abiding presence within us. We need to learn to be attuned to our inner centre: God's dwelling.

Sit down alone in a quiet room. Close your eyes and focus on looking inward. How do you visualise your deepest centre? Do you have an image or symbol that would help you?

For example, it is like looking into a deep, dark well and at the bottom is a point of light. Feel yourself going downward toward the point of light. The point of light is your inner centre, the ground of your existence: rest there.

Or imagine yourself taking a lift from the 20th floor to the basement. Look inward. Push the button and feel the lift moving downward. Down, down slowly, further and further and at last it comes to a stop: be still and just rest at the bottom.

Read the creation story in chapters 1—2 of Genesis. Draw a picture following the sequence of the text, drawing each thing in sequence as God creates it. Begin with some symbol of God. You could draw the picture all at once or over a space of time. What has the exercise taught you? How are you present to what you have drawn?

God's today in the Old Testament

Bible reading

The Old Testament uses the word 'today' for being present to the reality of encountering God at this particular moment of time. In the Old Testament God speaks of the renewal of past events in the present through the word 'today', making them dynamically present for the current assembly of Israel. Below is a selection of texts as a teaching for encountering the present moment. The book of Deuteronomy is full of these references to 'today':

'The Lord our God made a covenant with us at Horeb. Not with our ancestors did the Lord make this covenant, but with us, who are all of us here alive today' (Deuteronomy 5:2–3).

'Keep these words that I am commanding you today in your heart' (Deuteronomy 6:6).

Often the texts are connected to remembering what God has done and is renewing in the present:

'Remember that you were a slave in the land of Egypt, and the Lord your God redeemed you; for this reason I lay this command upon you today' (Deuteronomy 15:15).

Spend some time with these texts. Let the message sink into your consciousness. What are they saying to you in the context of your life and choices?

Read Deuteronomy 11 with its many references to 'today'. Study first the text and its meaning for the sacred author. What is the teaching to Israel? Only then begin applying the meaning of the 'today' texts to your life. Have you received new insights? How do they relate to the teaching in this article? How will you apply them to your life?

Following this theme through the rest of the Old Testament and into the New Testament would be a valuable study.

The ground of our existence

Reflective

The 'ground' of our existence is the deepest point of the human person and the place where God dwells. Thus our ground is also the divine ground.

To say a person is grounded means that he or she has a good understanding of what is really important in life. In a spiritual sense to be grounded is to be rooted in God. Awareness and understanding of the ground of our existence is to understand our nature and truth as human beings. It is in the ground of our existence that we touch God.

The secret of living in the present moment—being present to God in the eternal moment of time (which is the definition of the present moment)—is finding our inner centre. Stillness, listening and silence are the essential components for finding our centre and living in the present moment. The gift of the Holy Spirit within us teaches us and draws us into God.

'And I will ask the Father, and he will give you another Advocate, to be with you forever. This is the Spirit of truth, whom the world cannot receive, because it neither sees him nor knows him. You know him, because he abides with you, and he will be in you' (John 14:16–17).

To pray unceasingly is prayer of the heart. To pray from the heart is the habit of being in God's presence at every moment. It is a continual disposition to be in God that we can access throughout our day.

1. Reflect on the teaching presented in this section.
2. Make an outline of the teaching. Think through the various points.
3. How does the scripture text affirm the teaching?
4. What does it mean for you to live in the present moment?

5. Are you aware of God's presence with you during the day?
6. What do you need in order to become more aware of God's nearness?

Now: the intersection of time and eternity

Going out

We carry eternity in the deepest core of our heart, in the ground of our soul. This intersection of eternity and time is the 'now' of God. In the 'now' of God time and eternity intersect. When we live from our divine ground we experience this meeting of eternity with time. We are living in God's time.

Go to an open field or another large space. Stand in the middle with your hands at your side and feel your rootedness. Think of yourself as standing in the present moment without past or future. You are standing in the 'now' of God without beginning or end. Imagine your spirit expanding to infinite dimensions. Ask God for one word to describe what you are experiencing. Just be there silent and listening for about five minutes or longer.

Holy Spirit help me to find and dwell in my deepest centre, the ground of my being. Let it be for me a space of solitude that I can access even on the busiest of days. Give me the grace to live in the present moment: the 'now' of God. Teach me to be in God's will and filled with love. Open my heart to your transforming power. Amen

God's presence

Visual/creative

Entering into our ground of existence is at the same time to have entered into the heart of God. In our deepest centre we stand before God beyond words—in an essential relationship of love. In the ground of our existence we are face to face with God: essence to essence. God is there and we are there in the essential truth of our being. There are no words or thoughts, only silence and a knowing beyond knowing.

Pray over the above paragraph: try to visualise a symbol or a picture that expresses this profound experience of being present to and in God.

Draw a picture of a desert, using only one colour—a scene of sand stretching into infinity. In the middle of the picture draw two flowers facing one another. Ponder the effect the picture has on you as you create it and when it is finished.

Conclusion

Reflective

Living in the present moment, finding God in the present moment is not a complicated or impossible task. It is a matter of our daily choices, the development of habits and the openness of our heart to receive God, being people of prayer—being contemplative. Living a deeply contemplative life does not divorce us from living a practical life of virtue in the everyday circumstances of our lives.

By living with God in the present moment we enter into union with Jesus Christ, the Word of God—we become the place of God's salvation for all God's people and all created reality. Freedom and joy are the characteristics of a heart filled with God. Our society, to be healthy, needs men and women of integrity, committed people of faith who witness not only by what they say but primarily by the way they live their lives. The God from whom we come and toward whom we journey is the God who loves and asks us to love in concrete ways.

Reflect on the following checklist of practices that are a means to living in the present moment:

- Do less—put space between projects
- Stop worrying about the future—focus on the now
- When you're talking to someone, be present
- Avoid always multi-tasking. Do one thing at a time. When you eat, just eat, and so on
- Do what you are doing slowly and consciously
- Take time for your tasks—schedule less into your day
- Be a searcher
- Deepen your awareness of the reality about you; be present to that reality
- Reflect on and question life—we are meant to be questioners
- In all things seek God

The first letter to Timothy

Sally Smith

Who was Timothy?

Introduction

1 Timothy is the first of two letters addressed to Timothy who was a leader of the church, probably in Ephesus. It forms, along with 2 Timothy and Titus, what are known as the pastoral letters. The letters to Timothy are reputed to have been written by Paul, but there is considerable academic argument about whether this was the case or if they were written using some of his words, or even written by someone else altogether. We're not going to explore this here, but will assume this one is from Paul. Unlike most of the other epistles it was written not to a church, but to an individual person. Thomas Aquinas (1225–74) described 1 Timothy as a 'pastoral textbook' and if we read it with that in mind it begins to make more sense.

Timothy was a young man and in this letter he is being given advice about leadership and his role and lifestyle as a leader. It tends to move between several themes in a slightly haphazard way, and includes quotes from hymns and prayers that were likely to have been used at the time. The letter is specific to the situation in which Timothy was serving, but it also includes generalisations that could, and still can, be applied elsewhere. The three main themes that are woven throughout the letter are about countering false teachings in the church, instructions about church worship and the character of leaders and how they can be good servants of Christ.

I suggest you start by making a cup of tea or coffee and settling down somewhere comfortable to read the letter right through. You might prefer to print it out (you can easily print from websites such as biblegateway.com) and read it as if it were a letter that has arrived in the post for you, remembering that is what it was, a letter written for an individual to read on its own rather than as part of a larger book. So, settle down and read, being open to accepting passages that speak directly to you. Where you find Timothy's name replace it with your own name. Allow yourself to linger over some sections, and read other sections quickly.

When you have finished fold your letter (or close your Bible) and write your letter back to Paul. What do you want to thank him for? What do you want to argue with him about? What has struck you as important for you all these centuries later? What questions do you have?

Grace and mercy for all

Creative

In chapter 1 there is a very clear reminder to Timothy of Paul's former life, of how unsuitable he had been for the life he was now living, describing himself as the foremost of sinners. He recalls the qualities of a God who is able to forgive even him and how he can now be an example to others. That same grace and mercy that overflow for Paul are available for all of us.

I invite you to take some string or wool, a couple of metres would be fine. Roll it into a small neat ball. This is the person God would have you be.

Unravel the wool/string, scrunch it up and begin to tie it in knots (not too tight as you'll be trying to undo them again soon). As you tie and muddle the thread, think of the ways in which you have muddled up your life, the times you have not followed Christ and you have made a mess of things.

Look at the mess you have made. Imagine sitting or standing with God, and hear what he has to say about what you have done, both with the wool and with your life.

Then, gently, together, begin to unravel the mess. Begin to reform that small ball. Untie the knots, aware of God's patience with you as, together, you gently put it right. Notice his love and mercy for you as you work.

When you finally have your ball of wool or string back, notice how it may be different from how it started. Thank God for his persistence.

'To the King of the ages, immortal, invisible, the only God, be honour and glory for ever and ever, Amen' (1:17, NRSV).

Timothy—man of God

Background

As we read the letter, Paul lets us know what he thinks of Timothy and how much he values and trusts him. In 1:2 he describes him as 'my loyal child in the faith' or as THE MESSAGE says, 'my son in the faith'. Paul obviously feels he has helped Timothy grow in his faith and he was probably very influential in Timothy becoming a Christian in the first place. Again in 1:18 he calls him 'my child' and reminds him of prophecies made about Timothy which the teaching in the letter addresses. Paul trusts Timothy to carry on, knowing he will remain true to the good news and will continue to teach the truth. Timothy will need to draw on the groundwork that has already been done in him, the sound teaching he has received (presumably from Paul) that he has followed and which has brought him to this place where he can help others along their journeys. He encourages Timothy to continue teaching the people entrusted to him, 'If you put these instructions before the brothers and sisters, you will be a good servant of Christ Jesus' (4:6).

Paul has recognised the gift Timothy has (4:14) which was given through the laying on of hands, and he reminds Timothy not to neglect what God has given him.

We get the sense of Timothy as a man who has been nurtured in the church, who has been called to a specific ministry and has been faithful in following that call. He has been given the gifts and qualities he needs to fulfil that call.

Paul ends by reminding Timothy to 'guard what has been entrusted to you' (6:20) and praying for grace to be with him.

Who have been the people influential in making you the Christian you are today? What might they say if they were to write a letter to you?

Qualities of leaders

Creative/intercession

In chapter 3 Paul gives us a list of qualities to look for in leaders of the church. The NRSV uses the word 'bishops' implying senior overseers of the church. THE MESSAGE uses 'leader' opening it to a wider audience. Then from verse 8 there is a list of the qualities for 'deacons' (NRSV), 'servants' (THE MESSAGE) or 'helpers' (Good News). There is much overlap with these two lists. There is another similar list in Titus 1:6–9 (the third pastoral letter, also from Paul).

Take a piece of paper, or use a couple of pages in your journal to make some lists, side by side. First find and list the qualities required of bishops from 3:1–7.

Then match this with the list of qualities for deacons or helpers from 3:8–13, adding any new qualities mentioned at the end of your list.

Now look at Titus 1:6–9. Again match the qualities where you can and add any new ones to the end of your list.

As you prepare your lists, what do you notice? Are there some things which occur in all three lists; are there any surprises in what isn't included in all or any of the lists? How might these reflect the culture of the time and the situation Paul was addressing in which Timothy was working in Ephesus?

Now create a further list of the qualities and characteristics you would look for in a leader of the church today. Consider church leaders you know. Pray for them in the light of your list for church leaders today. Are there areas they particularly need God's help with? Are there areas in which you can support them, or encourage, thank or praise them for?

Now consider yourself. Whether you consider yourself to be a leader in the church or not, think about the qualities you do have—both those on the lists already and the many others you will have. How do these fit with your role in your church? Are there other characteristics you feel it would be good to have to enable you to undertake your service to the church? Hold the qualities you have and the qualities you feel you need before God, thanking him for his generous provision for you and for the work he has been doing in you over the years to bring you to this point, with these qualities that he can use in this way.

'Let a woman learn'

Reflective

1 Timothy 2 is frequently used to argue the place women should take in the church. It is highly controversial in its clear statement

that women should not teach and should be in submission. In Ephesus (where we are assuming Timothy was based) the main religion was a cult centred around the Temple of Artemis, which was a women-only cult, with only women priests. This had been a strong influence on the attitudes to women and men in the town, and Timothy had to deal with this influence. For the people of Ephesus there needed to be a change in the way they viewed women and men. Women, therefore, were to be encouraged to learn and to submit, not to their husbands, or to other men, but to God. They needed to be prepared for what lay ahead for them, and to learn well was, for Paul, a significant part of that process. Paul is countering a culture where women ruled strongly against men. He was emphasising that there was another way that the people of Ephesus could learn and embrace, and that it was both women and men who needed to learn new ways.

In this passage Paul is very clear that women should learn. Learning was not as common then as it is today, and people did not have access to the same resources for learning we have. How much do you value learning? How much time do you spend learning more about your faith and the God you follow? If you haven't done so recently, try reading a book to learn more, or listening to a talk (the internet is a good place to start learning; search for your favourite speaker or writer). Or if you have read or listened to someone recently, pause and reflect on what you learned from that book or person. How has this impacted on your faith and your service of God? If it has had no impact, do you need to revisit it?

Thanksgiving

Reflective

For everything created by God is good and nothing is to be rejected, provided it is received with thanksgiving; for it is sanctified by God's word and by prayer (4:4–5).

It is easy to see the world in simplistic terms—everything God made is good and everything else is bad. We all know there is a huge *but* to be added there. My kitchen knife is good while it is being used to prepare tonight's meal, but it is bad if it is used to attack the next person to walk past my house; my ability to use words is good when it is used to argue the case for someone in need, but not so good when it is used to belittle someone else. We can use God's creation and gift for his glory or for our own purposes.

Paul explores this idea further in 1 Corinthians 8—10 which he ends by summing up like this: 'So, whether you eat or drink, or whatever you do, do everything for the glory of God' (1 Corinthians 10:31). Pause and think about the things you have done in the past hour. You might like to begin trying to make a list of them all.

Now look at the list. How many of those things gave glory to God. Ask yourself, 'Could I stand before God and be proud of having acted in this way?' Which did not bring glory to God?—be honest with yourself and with God—he knows where his glory had been shown.

Now look forward to the next hour (or the first hour tomorrow morning) and the things you might be doing. What are you going to do that will intentionally bring glory to God? What are you going to do that you could make bring glory to God? Sanctify that hour by offering it in prayer to God and then go and live that hour to give God glory.

Christian living

Imaginative

Paul describes the characteristics of leaders within the church, basically saying they must be above reproach. We make the same demands on our leaders in society. Think of recent reports of people in the news whose private lives have become the headlines when they have behaved in less than perfect ways. As Christians we accept that no one is perfect, that we will all make mistakes. So why is Paul expecting such high standards from the leaders of the early church? The rest of us are human as well and if we are to trust and follow a leader, we need to believe that they are living the life, giving an example to follow and showing by their lives as well as by their teaching what Christ calls us to live out. But this role should not be left to the leaders. Each of us is an example of Christian living to those around us, those we meet regularly. We are called to be the example of Christ as well as to share his teaching with others.

I wonder how your neighbours (the people who live next door to you) view you. If they were to move and new people were to move in, I wonder what your current neighbours would say to your new neighbours about you. Imagine what that conversation might sound like? What might they not say? Imagine Jesus listening to that conversation with you. What saddens him about what you hear, and what does he rejoice over? What would you like to change in the light of what you have overheard?

The heavenly and the earthly

Prayer

> *He was revealed in flesh,*
>   *vindicated in spirit,*
> *seen by angels,*
>   *proclaimed among Gentiles,*
> *believed in throughout the world,*
>   *taken up in glory (3:16).*

Paul is describing the mystery of our faith. He refers to it in 3:9 when declaring deacons must 'hold fast to the mystery of the faith with a clear conscience'. This verse (3:16) may well have originally been a Christian hymn. The lines fit in pairs, with each pair describing both Christ on earth and the heavenly Christ (though set out differently in different versions). In 1 Peter 3:18 we read that Christ was 'put to death in the flesh, but made alive in the spirit'. He is both living with the angels and being preached among the nations, not just in the past of the first century, but in the present across the world. Christ, having been raised in glory, is ruling the world.

In similar ways we are part, not just of our earthly churches and communities but also part of the heavenly community with Christ. We are part of 'the household of God, which is the church of the living God' (3:15). Try making these lines into your prayer. Change the wording so you are addressing Jesus and proclaiming the mystery of your faith: 'You were revealed in flesh...'. Continue the prayer by proclaiming who Christ is for you, and if you can, add the corresponding earthly/heavenly description: 'You are my constant companion sitting at the right hand of the father.'

You may want to spend some time with these mysteries, allowing them to reveal to you more of your God.

Conforming or not

Creative

Tom Wright (*Paul for Everyone*, SPCK, 2004) argues that in chapter 3 Paul is saying we don't need to conform to the gender stereotyping of our age. As a massive generalisation, men at the time Paul was writing were prone to anger and arguments and women to dressing immodestly, with as much gold and decoration and expense as possible. But neither gender needed to be held by these stereotypes; each person was to be free to be the person God had made them to be and then to reflect their life following Christ in the way they behaved.

In what ways do you conform to the cultural gender stereotypes of our age? Pause and look back at the last few days and question why you acted in the way you did—was there anything you did because that was what was expected of you as a woman/man? Is there anything you would have preferred to have done differently, but that you feel may not have been seen as acceptable behaviour because of who you are? What might have happened if you had behaved differently—in terms of other people, yourself and God? It may be that you are comfortable with all you have done, believing you have acted as the person God intends you to be. Give thanks to him for the freedom to become that person and to serve him as yourself.

In what ways do you conform to the ways your culture demands? Take a magazine—one from the weekend papers would be good. Look through and notice how your lifestyle reflects what is portrayed and how it differs. Don't judge yourself but allow God to point to any areas where you could change.

Exercise

Reflective

'Train yourself in godliness' (4:7).

I lose count of the number of times I have made a decision to get fit. I've made a plan, decided what exercise I'll do and how often. I've signed up for the gym, pumped up the bike tyres… and then two weeks later, life has taken over and I'm not keeping to the plan and I'm no fitter. Sometimes we have a specific reason for getting fit—a desire to lose weight or to get fit enough to undertake a specific task (climb a mountain, walk, go on holiday). It's those times when we are more successful, when there's a definite timescale and measurable targets. Here Paul suggests that physical exercise (and fitness) has limited benefit and usefulness but that spiritual exercise is 'valuable in every way'. Spiritual health has benefits both in this world and in the life to come.

As with physical exercise, I have many times set out to get spiritually fit. I have made my plans, created a prayer space, bought a new prayer journal… and, as with the physical exercise, I find that two weeks later…

So, what have I learnt?

I need to have realistic expectations—to aim to do something I will be able to achieve—knowing that anything additional to this is a bonus.

I need a deadline and a reason for doing it. I need to know I am achieving and progressing. It is no accident that St Ignatius called his prayer retreat for new Christians 'The Spiritual Exercises'. They are structured and develop over 30 days as the retreatant practises and develops in new ways and habits, but they need perseverance and the support of a good companion to continue.

We are all different. You will have different motivations. Pause and see if you can find what has helped you succeed in the past, whether that is in spiritual, physical or other projects. What motivates you? What helps you keep going? It may be that you need to commit to something in the presence of someone else, making your intentions known and then be held to your promise. Or you may need not to have a plan at all, but just the decision to change. You may need visual reminders, notes or objects in places where you will see or feel them.

Then consider: what are you expecting to gain from your spiritual life? Ask God to help you achieve that. Make your decisions. How does this help you achieve what you are aiming for?

Personal instruction

Creative

As well as being a handbook on church leadership, 1 Timothy is a personal letter from Paul to Timothy, and so includes some personal advice on how he is to look after himself, like the command to drink some wine 'for the sake of your stomach and your frequent ailments' (5:23). This is the advice from an older to a younger man, passing on his gained wisdom and showing his concern for the younger.

If 4:6–16 were to be written to me, they may begin:

'If you do what you have been asked to do, you will be a good servant of Christ, but you need to feed on the words you have heard and follow the teaching you have been given. Don't get side-tracked with gossip, but remain focused on God...'

If these verses were to be written to you, what would they say? Try rewriting this passage making it relevant to your situation.

As you write receive the promises and instructions held within these verses for you.

When you have finished, reread what you have written.

How do you respond to God?

Leaving Timothy and Paul

Creative

To end your time with Timothy and Paul, why not take your folded letter (or Bible) and return to the place where you originally read the letter. Open your paper or Bible and begin reading, this time with the insights and encounters you have gained. If you have printed a copy you might want to add notes in the margins as you read, or to highlight different verses or words. Pause over phrases and recall what they have meant for you, what you have learned, and how you are going to take that knowledge or experience on into the next weeks and months.

'And oh, my dear Timothy, guard the treasure you were given! Guard it with your life... People caught up in a lot of talk can miss the whole point of faith. Overwhelming grace keep you!' (6:20–21, *THE MESSAGE*).

Into the desert

Liz Hoare

Introduction

Visual

The desert is integral to biblical spirituality. Indeed it is inconceivable to imagine the world of the Bible without it. Every great event, every towering personality in scripture is shaped by the desert, or wilderness as it is also known. Deuteronomy 32:10–14 is a picture of how God worked in the desert context to form his people.

Think about the impact of the landscape on the way you have been formed. Did you grow up with lots of noise in a large family where mealtimes were talkative occasions or was there a lot of quiet at home? Were you bought up in a busy city or a remote village? What were the key formative features of your early life?

Words associated with the desert include barren, dry, waste-land, deserted. What other words would you use to describe a desert place?

What about images of the desert? Perhaps you have enjoyed films such as *Lawrence of Arabia* or *The English Patient*, but there are many kinds of desert on our planet. As you explore the desert, you might find it helpful to collect some pictures of deserts and wilderness spaces. They will probably not all be images of vast sand dunes. Our towns and cities have their own deserts: patches of waste ground, bleak areas of concrete corridors which constantly funnel chill winds through them.

Deserts may be geographical spaces, but they are also states of mind. Most of us will have a 'wilderness' experience at some time in our lives. Prayer dries up and seems to go nowhere, God feels far away or absent altogether, or life seems joyless and barren. We may choose to retreat to the desert to seek God, but the desert also seeks us at times and comes unbidden.

Try drawing a geographical 'map' of your spiritual life. What are the key features of your internal landscape at present?

Read Psalm 42 and use the verses that echo your own situation to talk to the Lord.

The Bible and the desert

Spotlight

Someone has said that 'The God of the Bible is the God of the desert', for the desert is the place where God revealed himself to individuals and to the nation of Israel. Every significant leader was shaped in the desert: Abraham, Moses, Jacob, Elijah, the prophets, and in the New Testament: John the Baptist, St Paul and Jesus. It is not surprising that Christians have sought God in the desert, but perhaps more disturbing is the fact that the desert seeks us out too; sometimes the Holy Spirit propels us to a place that is profoundly uncomfortable and seemingly far away from God and the life he promises. It is important to notice that the Bible does not begin nor does it end in the desert, but the desert certainly plays a significant role in between.

The desert was an important part of Jesus' life and provides the clue to what it's all about. Having grown up in obscurity Jesus' ministry was preceded by 40 days and nights in the desert where he was tempted by Satan to do things in his own way rather than God's. During his ministry he sought out lonely places to pray and he encouraged his disciples to accompany him to such places.

Different words are used in Greek to describe the places

Jesus chose to be alone with his heavenly father. For example, Mark 1:45 says 'Jesus stayed out in the country' (*eremos*—an abandoned, empty, solitary place), while Luke 5:15–16 refers to 'deserted places' (NRSV) or 'lonely places' (NIV).

Do you have a 'desert place' to steal away to and be alone with God? Could you go there to spend some time alone with God? If it's too far or you don't have a special place, could you create one close to home? A single chair in a special place would do.

Praying in the desert

Prayer

The purpose of solitude and freedom from distractions in the wilderness is to leave room for prayer, the heart of our relationship with God. This is why Jesus sought lonely places to spend time with his heavenly father. But how do we pray when part of the desert experience is the feeling that God is not listening? The way that the desert fathers and mothers learned to pray is as relevant today as it was then and can be followed anywhere. First of all they prayed the psalms, repeating them and meditating on them. This meant that they covered the whole range of human experience as it is present in the Psalter: from praise to lament, longing to overflowing joy, rage to quiet rest like a weaned child. They learned them by heart and recited them aloud as they prayed, and slowly the words entered into the fabric of their being.

Which psalms are especially familiar to you? Consider the emotions expressed and which ones especially resonate with you at the moment. Try to learn a psalm as you focus on the desert. Psalm 63 is not too long and uses imagery connected with the desert. Another important prayer principle learned in the desert is that God does not need elaborate words when we cry out to him. Macarius the Great, one of the desert fathers, was asked, 'How should one pray?' The old man answered: 'There is no need to make long discourses. It is enough to stretch out one's hands and say: "Lord, as you will and as you know, have mercy." And if the conflict presses further say, "Lord, help me." He knows very well what we need and he shows us his mercy.' Simplicity in prayer is a wonderful gift. 'Your father knows what you need' so cry to him (Matthew 6:8). John Cassian was a monk who brought the sayings of the desert to the Western Church and learned how to pray from the desert dwellers. His favourite prayer was, 'O Lord make speed to save us; O Lord make haste to help us' which passed into Benedictine tradition and then into the Book of Common Prayer. Praying short prayers like this, especially if prayed aloud, can help us move from the voice to the mind and then to the heart, and so involve the whole of us. Other short prayers include 'Come, Lord Jesus!' (Revelation 22:20), 'Hear my cry, O God' (Psalm 61:1), and 'Lead me, O Lord' (Psalm 5:8).

Spend some of your prayer time today using short, simple prayers to your heavenly father. If you only have a short time for this section today carry over the practice of short arrow prayers into your tasks.

Moses meets God at Horeb

Bible reading

Read Exodus 3:1–6, 11–14.

Moses had fled from Egypt, where he had been important, to Midian, where he was nobody. He spent 40 years here keeping someone else's sheep which meant wandering to look for fresh pasture. Moses needed the busyness and prestige of Pharaoh's household to be emptied out of him in order to be filled with the presence of the Lord. It was doubtless a humbling experience but that does not mean it must have been all negative. He must have had a great deal of time to think, to learn to observe, to listen, to ponder the meaning of things. When he was ready, God met him in an extraordinary way, using something ordinary—a bush.

Notice the following: first, God called him by name. We may feel stripped bare in the desert, but God knows us by name. The desert may be the place where we find our true identity as beloved (compare Isaiah 43:1). Next, when Moses 'turned aside' to look, God spoke to him. We may need the desert to help us let go of distractions that block out God's voice. Then God told Moses to take off his shoes for he was standing on holy ground. To take off our shoes is to become vulnerable. It is more difficult to run away. It also acknowledges that God is holy. What has been holy ground for you in your life?

God said: 'I am the God of your father, the God of Abraham, the God of Isaac and the God of Jacob' (v. 6) and thus linked Moses with his past. God made a covenant with Abraham and was faithful to each of the patriarchs. Their stories were interwoven with God's purposes and they found him to be trustworthy. What is important for you to remember and hold fast to from your faith community?

Moses needed the 40 years in the desert to prepare him to meet God and respond to him at Horeb. Have you been conscious that the dry times of your Christian experience have prepared you for the next step in life?

Ask God to call you by name as he did Moses; physically turn away from distractions—perhaps face a blank wall. Take off your shoes—feel the surface below. Listen, to the one who is God before whom you stand. 'I am the God…'; allow God to finish the sentence.

A survivor's guide to the desert

Reflective

The early Christians referred to themselves as 'resident aliens' *paroikoi, xenoi* in Greek, *peregrini* in Latin, to denote that they were not at home in this world but were seeking 'a better country, that is, a heavenly one' (Hebrews 11:16). As Christianity changed from being persecuted to being the acceptable face of the Roman Empire, growing numbers of believers left the comfort of the cities to move into the desert to seek God for himself alone. One of the most famous was St Antony of Egypt who responded to the words of Matthew 19:21: 'If you wish to be perfect, go, sell your possessions, and give the money to the poor... then come, follow me.' Antony lived in the desert as a hermit while others lived in small communities. Antony's guidance was often sought after by others who wanted to know more of God. The lives and sayings of people like Antony have blessed and challenged Christians ever since and many are rediscovering their wisdom today.

The strange thing is that even in the desert people realised that they could not grow in grace without other people. Learning humility and freedom from selfishness and the need to justify ourselves constantly requires that we walk the Christian way alongside others, even when the road looks bare and uninviting. Rowan Williams explores this in his little book *Silence and Honey Cakes* and quotes the desert fathers saying: 'Salvation lies with our neighbour' (Rowan Williams, *Silence and Honey Cakes*, Lion, 2003, pp. 22ff).

What sustains you when life seems a barren place and prayer feels dry? Are there people in your life who refresh you in your deserts? Try drinking a glass of clear, cold water and as you feel it go down, recall someone who has spoken words of refreshment that have revived and reinvigorated you.

Spend some time giving thanks for the people, activities and places that refresh you.

The desert and solitude

Going out

Desert spirituality is the precise opposite of marketplace spirituality. The latter is busy, full of activity and choices, so many choices that we never really put down roots that will refresh us when the tough times come. The primary call of the desert is to be with God and to seek him for himself alone. This will always be a challenge, but perhaps never more so than today when an ever-increasing array of distractions threaten to choke the life from us. Deliberately walking away may be the only way to still the ceaseless activity both inward and outward.

In the desert, there is little or no activity, at least at first. We are just waiting; there are few choices, we sit in our 'cell' doing nothing. Spiritual dryness can come out of the blue and it is a lonely experience.

We feel isolated inside and the dryness suggests that even God has abandoned us. There is a world of difference between loneliness and solitude, however, and the desert can help us discover the delight of being alone with God in peaceful solitude.

Take a walk to a wilderness place, leaving your phone at home. Your 'wilderness' may be in the city centre rather than a riverside path, but the point of this solitary walk is not to revel in a beautiful landscape but to be alone with God, to listen for his voice. Notice the emptiness and the feelings this creates inside you. Speak to the Lord about the deserts of your own soul, but also allow time for your busy thoughts to settle and be still. Keep coming back to a simple word or phrase such as 'Be still and know' or 'Fill me, Lord' each time you recognise that your mind has wandered again.

Jesus and his temptations in the wilderness

Bible study

Read Mark 1:12, 13.

Given its significance in the way people were shaped by the desert, it is perhaps not surprising that Jesus himself spent a formative period of time there. Immediately following his baptism, Mark tells us that the Spirit drove him out into the wilderness where for 40 days he was tempted by Satan. Mark also tells us that he was with the wild beasts and the angels waited on him. In these two short verses there is a great deal to ponder, especially in the light of the Old Testament stories of the desert experience.

We probably imagine the desert to be an empty place, devoid of life of any kind because of the lack of water. Yet there are many creatures in the wilderness. Jesus encountered Satan and the character of his future life and ministry was hammered out. He also knew God's kindness through the ministry of the angels, his messengers. But what of the wild beasts? There are many stories of the desert fathers and their relationship with the creatures that inhabited the desert. They show a world where there was friendship between humans and wild beasts such as lions, wolves and crocodiles. Together they signified the new world order initiated by the redemption Christ wrought on the cross. When Mark says that in the desert Jesus was 'with the wild beasts' (Mark 1:13), he is telling us that the new world has begun and humans are being recalled to their original task of honouring God in and with all creation. Jesus, the new Adam, restores the broken relationships caused by the sin of the first Adam and one day we will take our proper place in the world as living signs of God's grace and stewards of creation (Romans 8:18–30). Meanwhile there are wild beasts that seek to catch us out (1 Peter 5:8) and we need to be watchful. Macarius the Great talked of 'dragons' in the human heart as well as the treasures of grace. Like Jesus, the desert fathers expected to encounter evil in the desert and spiritual warfare was part of their calling.

What are the 'dragons' that beset you in the desert places of your heart? What spiritual weapons are available to you to overcome them?

The desert and silence

Reflective

Silence is inextricably linked with the desert experience. For some people silence is a gift, but for others it is a curse. Some of us long for stillness and silence to free us from the distractions of noise and endless activity, but for others it signals loneliness and isolation, even the sense that God has abandoned them.

As human beings we need silence in our lives just as we need community and the companionship of others. To long for silence does not mean that we are trying to evade the world around us. Jesus went away from the crowds to a lonely place while remaining totally committed to his mission to the world. If the Church today is to respond to the world as God wants and not as our programmes dictate, we must learn to be still in order to hear what God is saying. 'The wind blows where it chooses' (John 3:8) but can we hear?

For the desert fathers and mothers silence was less a replacement for words than something that enabled words to recover their power. They sought silence not for its own sake, but in order to be able to hear God speaking. In a society where words come cheap and are often abused, the silence of the desert could help us speak in such a way that the living word could once again be heard afresh.

What part does silence have in the life of your church? Where does it occur when the community gathers together?

Where does silence occur in your day? You may live alone and long for someone to talk to, but for many of us, silence is hard to achieve. Even when we find silence on the outside, the inward chatter of our minds seems impossible to still. Try to build some silence into your day this week. Switch off your mobile devices, go for a solitary walk or find a quiet room and look out of the window or at some favourite pictures with no agenda other than to notice what you see. You could use the pictures you have collected of desert places.

The spiritual desert of dryness and emptiness

Imaginative

In 1 Kings 19 Elijah the prophet had a desert experience that was both literal and spiritual. Fleeing from the wrath of Queen Jezebel following his triumph on Mount Carmel, he collapsed under a broom tree and prayed to die. He felt a total failure and all perspective was lost to him. But God had not finished with his servant and, having fortified him with food and rest, he met him at Horeb and recommissioned him for service.

Allow the scene to take shape in your mind's eye. Using the five senses, build up a picture of Elijah under the broom tree, broken and asking to die. Hear his prayer of despair and watch him fall asleep. Picture the hand of the angel touching him (is it a gentle stroke or a vigorous shake?) and hear the command to arise and eat. Imagine the rest of this scene and then the difference as after the second meal Elijah runs the great distance before him and comes to the holy mountain. Imagine him retreating to his cave and then the voice of God questioning him: 'What are you doing here, Elijah?' See Elijah going out onto the mountainside while the Lord passed by. Take time to feel the impact of the powerful wind, then an earthquake and then a raging fire. Finally comes a 'still small voice' (KJV) or 'a sound of sheer silence' (NRSV). Which is it? Do you react like Elijah and wrap your face in your coat? Hear God's question the second time and Elijah's exact same response. What is God saying to you? And how will you respond?

The spirituality of the desert

Reflective

One of the key features of the desert is the way it slows us down. Waiting is anathema to our instant culture, yet in the desert there is often nothing else to do but wait. The desert fathers said: 'Go to your cell and your cell will teach you everything.' Nothing happens fast in the desert and we are forced learn to do things in God's time rather than ours. When our demand for instant gratification spills over into our walk with God we expect immediate answers to prayer every time, no-effort discipleship and painless transformation into the likeness of Christ. In contrast, the Bible commands again and again that we 'wait for the Lord' and that waiting may be a very long time. We need resources to help us to wait patiently and in trust, not losing hope or sight of God's promised future. The watchword of the desert was 'maranatha', for the desert fathers and mothers were watching and waiting for signs of the coming of the kingdom of God. They wanted to be ready.

Along with waiting come other features that characterise desert spirituality, one of which is stripping off all that hinders. In the film *Lawrence of Arabia* there is a scene where a man crosses the desert in blistering heat and one by one he drops the things that weigh him down. In the desert we are stripped bare. This leads to humility, another key quality of the lives of the desert fathers and mothers. They refused to judge others because they became more aware of their own shortcomings. They also valued simplicity and the importance of faithfully doing the next thing.

What is the desert inviting you to put down in order to move forward with God?

Read Micah 7:7 and reflect on the experience of waiting expectantly.

Choosing the desert

Creative

We may not be able to down tools and head off to a desert place to be alone with God, and the desert stories of the Bible may seem remote from the landscapes we are used to. One of the most creative ways of engaging with the Bible of recent times that involves more than thinking about it is Godly Play®. Many of the stories recreated through Godly Play involve a 'desert box' which, as the name suggests, is a box filled with sand to represent the desert landscape in which the major events of the Bible took place. There may be a Godly Play centre near you where you could borrow the equipment but you can easily buy sand for children's sandpits and construct your own desert. Pour some onto a tray, add some rocks and choose a Bible passage to work with. You may have some play figures to reconstruct the story or you could use clothes pegs or cut-out figures. Move them around the sand as you tell the story aloud slowly. Good ones to work with are Abram's journey through the Negev, Moses at Horeb encountering the burning bush, Elijah fleeing Queen Jezebel and meeting God on the mountain, or the tortuous journey into exile of the people of Israel.

'The desert shall rejoice and blossom'

Poetry

Isaiah 35 gives a wonderful picture of the transformation of the desert when the glory of the Lord comes to his people to restore and heal them. One of the disorientating things about the desert is the lack of landmarks and signposts. It is all too easy to get lost and see no end to the relentless barren terrain. God's silence, too, seems unending. Just as the Jewish and Christian faiths were born out of the desert, so renewal also comes from the wilderness wastes in which we find ourselves. Scripture reminds us that God led his people into the desert in order to shape them. It was there that they found their vocation to be his people, they received the Law and encountered the power of almighty God. It is out of the desert too that the Bible promises redemption and restoration. Isaiah 35 is a wonderful picture of what this will look like. The desert will blossom with life abundant, it will be clear which way to take and there will be joy-filled, exuberant life everywhere.

First note down the transformations that are promised when the Lord comes, then make a note of the difficulties that are on your mind at present. Which images speak to your situation with especial meaning? Try writing your own poem as a prayer of longing for God's renewal and restoration.

Look again at the pictures you have collected of the desert. Can you imagine what they would look like if they were to blossom in the way that Isaiah describes?

Hosea—a love story

Anne Noble

Background

Introduction

The prophet Hosea is one of twelve so-called minor prophets of the Old Testament. In 928BC the united kingdom of Israel split into a northern kingdom (Israel) and a southern (Judah) each with a succession of kings. Some of these kings were good, others 'did evil in the sight of the Lord', principally by allowing the worship of other gods, seeking alliances with foreign powers and doing little or nothing to counter injustice towards the most vulnerable in their lands. It is generally believed that Hosea was written to the northern kingdom of Israel from the latter years of the reign of King Jeroboam II in the years of political chaos that followed Jeroboam's death (746BC). During this time there was a rapid turnover of kings often following assassinations (for example, 7:7). This was a time of outside threat from both Egypt and Assyria and eventually Israel fell to the Assyrians in 722BC. Hosea writes against a background of national and international crisis to warn kings, priests and the people of the personal and national consequences of their unfaithfulness to God. As one commentator puts it, this was a time of life or death for the nation of Israel both spiritually and politically. As with all the prophets, Hosea's message is timeless, applying to individuals and nations throughout the ages.

Find a time to read the whole book of Hosea. Do not be surprised if you find it complex and are shocked by some of its imagery. Hosea does not mince his words which, written in the context of a patriarchal society, can sound especially harsh for women today. There are two opening metaphors. The first is marriage between an unfaithful woman,[1] Gomer, and the prophet Hosea. The second is the parenthood of three prophetically named children: Jezreel (God sows/plants), Lo-ruhamah (not pitied) and Lo-ammi (not my people). These metaphors, which underlie much of the text, stand for the relationship between God and his people. The relationship, which should be sacred, is broken and damaged by the unfaithfulness of the people. God is betrayed by Israel in its alliances with foreign nations and Israel is unfaithful to God in its worship of Baal (for example, 2:13) and by the practice of mixing Baal worship with that of God (2:16). At times the text boils with the anger of God.

And yet…

God also feels pain. We read of the struggle and even suffering within God between righteous anger which demands punishment and overwhelming grace and mercy which are his character and commitment to Israel. His love reaches out to them while they are still turning away from him (chapter 11). Beyond the coming disaster God speaks of the possibility of new life and new beginnings—images of a resurrection hope that overwhelms the grave. What is the nature of God revealed here? Do you always find yourself 'liking' God in these texts? Also think about how these words apply not just to individuals but to whole communities and even countries. You might find it helpful to read Hosea and then read a national paper.

However provocative you find the text, try to stay with it— though take care of yourself if the images used in Hosea stir

---

1. The NRSV translates the word here as 'whore' but the Hebrew refers more to adultery than to a profession.

painful memories. If this is true you may prefer to skip the next section, and avoid the first three chapters of Hosea.

God, your love for us never fails. As we read your word, may your encouragements lift us in our lives and your shocks stir us to come home to you.

A difficult metaphor—broken promises

Reflective

Read Hosea 1—3. As you read the chapters be aware of how they make you feel. If they come close to the bone of your personal experience make sure you have someone you can speak to about it.

The first three chapters of Hosea contain the underlying metaphor of the 'marriage' between Hosea and Gomer which stands for the relationship between God and Israel (here represented by Gomer). They are not an easy read, especially if you are a woman reading from the perspective of Gomer. We might find the shaming of Gomer to be abusive in a modern context. As a result some scholars, especially feminist critics, have found the image of God they present very difficult indeed. Other commentators argue that there is much that this metaphor brings to our understanding of the depth of God's love and what it costs God to love a people who consistently turn away from him.

God calls Hosea to marry an adulterous woman as an acted parable which exposes the relationship between God and his people Israel. The metaphor emphasises the depth of pain experienced by God as Israel pursues idolatry and foreign alliance, breaking the covenant relationship of love between them. God's love is spurned by Israel and sacred trust in them has been betrayed.

Verses 14–20 of chapter 2 speak of God's promise to woo Israel back into relationship. God initiates these words of restoration independently of any move from Israel to return to him. The language is that of a betrothal which not only restores the bond between God and his people in the most intimate of terms but also restores the land. You might like to compare Hosea 2:18–20 with the more well-known promises of Isaiah (11:1–9). Finally the children too are transformed by God's redeeming love with the change of their names.

Spend some time with this image of restoration. Perhaps you might like to read the parable of the prodigal son in Luke 15 and reflect with both of these on the priority of God's love which embraces and transforms those who return to him.

Forgiving God, you run to meet us in your son, and in your embrace is healing for all the times we turn away.

Broken promises

Creative

Has anyone ever made a promise to you and then deliberately broken it? How did that feel?

The following creative exercise uses something broken to make something new, which represents the cost of God's love. There are two ways to do this, either by breaking a ceramic object or by tearing up a beautiful picture.

Firstly, look out for some strong cardboard (such as that used in packing cases) or a piece of plywood. Cut a cross shape from this (or draw a large empty cross onto the plywood if you are unable to cut it). In a charity shop or perhaps from your own collection carefully break a piece of decorated china (an odd plate or coloured tiles) or tear up a beautiful picture taken from a magazine or perhaps an old photograph. (Be careful to protect yourself from cuts if you use a ceramic object and wear gloves to protect your hands—but imagine, if you like, what it would be like to experience the cuts.) Note how it feels to break or tear.

Using glue, make a mosaic on the cross outline using your broken or torn-up pieces. Try to make this as beautiful as you can. Take time over this and, if you are able, consider how God redeems the broken places of our lives. If there are places which are still raw, trust them to God and know his presence in the suffering as well as in the healing. Don't worry if there are gaps. You could either fill these with another picture or object or leave them for a later time in life. You might also like to fill them with coloured pieces representing times of healing.

This project may take some time. When you have finished place your cross where you can see it. If you have chosen to make your cross from pieces of ceramic mounted on a wooden board then you might like to finish it by grouting them in place.

God, broken in Jesus on the cross, sometimes it is difficult to understand how you love us, sometimes impossible. Help us to know that your love can make broken places whole.

A lament of broken promises

Prayer

With your mosaic cross in front of you, pray the following lament. If you didn't make this in the previous section you could use a picture of Jesus on the cross instead. You might like to add lines of your own.

If faithfulness ends in betrayal
If truth turns to dishonesty
If love is replaced by hate
If tenderness is returned in violence
If promises end in brokenness
then

I cry to you in my pain.

O God, I know you understand what it is to suffer; your cross shouts to a fractured world that you do. I know you know what it is to be broken, betrayed and bruised—all this I am told, but in the face of the agony help me to believe that it is true.

Remain before the cross with its brokenness and yours. Know that Christ is with you in the pain. Know too that he bears it for you. Stay with this for as long as you feel able. If you need to, find a trusted person to talk with about your experience.

Charge and confession

Prayer

Read Hosea 4:1–3.

As you read notice the sins of omission that Hosea cites as well as the sins of commission. You might also notice how these recall the ten commandments.

God brings a charge against his people which is harsh in both content and also in its scope—it is against the inhabitants of the land, the whole community, and though Hosea will go on to single out priests and rulers for special mention, here all of us are in view. The people have not been faithful or merciful and they have no knowledge of God. The result is swearing, lying, murder, stealing and adultery. The sins of omission echo the positive commandments to put God first and love him whilst the sins of commission echo the commandments that deal with our relationships with one another. The result is bloodshed and chaos in society and the withering/mourning of the land. All creation suffers when humankind has its theological priorities wrong: sin has its consequences.

It is uncomfortable reading. However, as we shall see later in our study, all is not lost. For as Christians we always have the view of a gracious loving God in mind and the offer of forgiveness, especially as it is extended through Jesus on the cross. Hope lies in the very nature of God and his promises to love his people.

The following confession (based on Hosea 4, Deuteronomy 6:4 and Mark 12:29–30) may help you to focus on specific areas of your life that you would like to bring before God.

Loving God, I have not always loved you with my whole heart or my neighbour as myself. Sometimes I have failed to love myself as well. Help me to love as you love me and when that is difficult, to want to love you more.

Faithful God, I have not always loved you with my whole soul, though you have given me my life and redeemed it. Help me to seek you with all that I am and, when that is difficult, to want to seek you more.

God of understanding, I have not always sought you with my whole might, though you have always been my rock and my strength. Help me to rely on you and, when that is difficult, to want to lean on you more.

Forgiveness: Read Mark 12:28–34 and concentrate on the words of Jesus to the scribe in verse 34: 'You are not far from the kingdom of God.' Know that God forgives you.

Hesed

Spotlight

One of the Hebrew words that lie behind the text of Hosea is *hesed,* which is difficult to translate into English and is often rendered as steadfast love by the NRSV. The issue at the heart of Hosea is that the faithful, steadfast love of God for his people, his *hesed,* has been spurned, and we read of God's pain at Israel's failure to respond with *hesed* towards God. The *hesed* of God is God's faithful commitment to his people. Its meaning carries a sense of kindness, faithfulness, mercy, generosity, forgiveness, reliability and loyalty which qualify judgement and lead to justice. *Hesed* continues despite any rejection they might make. There is a generosity and grace in *hesed* which means that it costs God to love the people in this way, a cost which we find ultimately paid on the cross by Jesus.

Spend some time today reflecting on God's *hesed* for you. How do you feel that God loves you in this way?

The ephemeral and the permanent

Creative

The beginning of Hosea 6 uses images of reliability and permanence to describe God's love for his people versus images of the transient to describe the people's love for God. We can know God is always there and is reliable, both daily and through the seasons of the year, though we perhaps take that for granted: sometimes as human beings our love for God comes and goes rather easily.

Humanly speaking it is difficult, if not impossible, to be fully aware of God's presence and return his love every second of every day (that's reserved for heaven!). However, we can help ourselves to be more aware of God and turn our thoughts to him, all of which help to build up our relationship with him.

Write the words of Hosea 6:3 onto Post-it notes or small pieces of paper. Place these in strategic places in your home and workplace that mark the passing of time; for example, diaries, calendars and clocks. They will be a reminder that God has promised to be present in all our times and seasons.

At the beginning of the day pray:

Lord, your love for us is as certain as the returning dawn—we know that it is new every morning and every day is filled with your fresh possibilities. Help us to be alive to that constantly.

Lord, our love for you sometimes evaporates in the heat of life. Help us to remember your presence through the activity of the day and to know that you are with us always.

Lord, your love for us is as reliable as the seasons—you promise to be there in all the turns of life even to the end of the age. Help us to become more aware of you in all the seasons of our lives.

Mercy not sacrifice

Creative

Jesus quotes Hosea 6:6 in the calling of Matthew as it is told in Matthew's Gospel (Matthew 9:9–13). Matthew alone of the Gospel writers places these words on Jesus' lips on this occasion. If the writer of the Gospel is Matthew himself then what was it about this verse that was so important to him? We may never know but I wonder whether it was the fact that Jesus was prepared to cross social boundaries to call to repentance and discipleship a tax-collector, a sinner and someone unclean in the eyes of the religious hierarchy of the day. Such is the boundary-crossing nature of God's love.

The temple sacrifices of that day were about maintaining purity and paying for the sins of the people. Jesus drew close to people, risking uncleanness in the process, in order to draw sinners close to himself. Mercy, for Jesus, was more desirable than sacrifice, because mercy can heal sinners who know their need of God.

In the famous court scene of *The Merchant of Venice* Shakespeare places these words on Portia's lips: 'The quality of mercy is not strain'd, it droppeth as the gentle rain from heaven upon the place beneath' (Act 4, scene 1).

Take a glass of water and some food colouring or ink. Carefully drop a small amount of the ink or colouring into the water and watch as it spreads out and changes the colour of the water. Now imagine the same effect in your life—God's mercy and forgiveness dropped into your life. Imagine, or perhaps remember how God can and has transformed your life, and be thankful.

God, your mercy changes me so that I can live in your presence forever. May I know that life now, spreading through all my being until I am filled with all the fullness of your love.

Trusting the wrong things

Imaginative

Chapter 8 outlines the core of the issue the Lord has with Israel. Israel has rejected its covenant relationship with God through the establishment of kings, the worship of idols and in forming alliances with foreign powers, specifically Assyria. The ram's horn sounds in 8:1 to bring the people to attention, to warn them and to announce God's presence; danger is hovering over them.

The whole chapter is God's warning to them about what they are doing and its consequences and there is a particularly sensory illustration of this in verse 7. If they sow (or sow in) the wind they will reap (reap in) the whirlwind. What farmer would risk precious seed by sowing it when the conditions were windy? Equally, what is the point in sowing emptiness? Israel has put its trust in empty power and gods which cannot deliver—the result will be a harvest of nothingness and what little yield there is will simply be devoured by the coming aggressors. God asks us to trust him even when the circumstances are difficult, perhaps even threatening.

Try to imagine this verse with all your senses: the sound of wind and whirlwind, the feel of grain in your hand being carried away by the wind, the disappointment when the harvest fails, the hunger pains in your stomach when there is no bread. Now imagine the reverse, the sowing of seed in good conditions, the succession of the seasons watching the grain grow and anticipating the harvest, the celebration of harvest home.

God, you trust us with your most precious gift of love; help us to treasure that gift so that it may grow in us in times of emptiness and abundance.

Cords of love

Creative

Read the description of God as parent in Hosea 11:1–11. The verses probably refer to God leading Israel out of Egypt in the Exodus (especially 4:22–23). The prophet's words remind the people of God's past faithfulness to them. They speak tenderly of God in the present moment, as a parent gently leading his children, perhaps even teaching them to walk. Yet this love and calling is rejected by Israel (vv. 6–7). God struggles to respond: 'How can I give you up?' (v. 8). Finally there is a future promise that God's power will restore the fortunes of Israel. They will be exiled as a punishment for their idolatry but God will call them back. In the end God's desire is to win people back (vv. 10–11).

Take three pieces of ribbon, wool or cord, knot them together at one end and begin to weave them into a plait. One strand represents you, another is time and the third is God. Do this slowly. Imagine weaving God into your life and times from as far back as you can remember until now. There will no doubt be times when you have felt especially close to God, and God to you, and others where you felt more distanced. Perhaps there have been times when you wondered where God was. Note these times. If you have some beads available you could thread them onto the individual strands as you note times of special closeness or distance (one colour for each).

Be sure to leave the plait unfinished—your story with God is not over yet.

Hold the plait in your open hands and look at its patterns of intertwined colours and beads. Can you see the pattern of God within your life? Does this surprise you? As you hold your time in your hands recall that God holds all your times and life in his hands. Look at the present moment—the place where the weaving stops. How are you with God right here and now? If you could say something to God in this moment what would it be? Finally the future lies as yet unwoven. Does this feel exciting or worrying? Give your future into God's hands and know that he will be woven into it just as he is into your past and present.

God of the past, present and future, you have called me into this life and you have woven your life and mine together in time. Keep me always close to you, and when I wander draw me gently back to you with cords of human kindness and bands of love.

Love hurts

Reflective

Read Hosea 11:5–11. In these verses we read of the coming exile that will result from Israel's turning away from God. Assyria will be their king, war will come upon them and it will consume them and their cities. Yet in the midst of this judgement God's voice is raised in lament. Verse 8 must rank as amongst the most poignant in the Bible as God appears to struggle with the requirements of his holiness (punishment for sin) and the love and compassion which is God's nature. We read: 'My heart recoils within me; my compassion grows warm and tender.' God is God and no mortal; he is the Holy One in their midst.

God does not give up on us when we fail. He may hate the sin but he loves the sinner and we are the recipients of his undeserved love.

Read these verses again. Hear how passionate God is for his people and how he struggles with them. Write a letter to God expressing what it means to hear that he loves you like this. Offer your letter as prayer.

Abundant life in God

Imaginative

Read chapters 12 and 13, which once again lay the complaint against Israel. Now read chapter 14. The words here are of the promise of the life which will follow from Israel's return. Israel has stumbled because of sin but God holds out a future that is characterised by abundance and growth.

Find a quiet space and read Hosea 14:4–8 slowly. As you do so, imagine the scene the verses depict. Try to use all your senses. See the trees as they grow, the strength in the trunks, the spreading canopy which offers shade and protection. Smell the fragrance of the lilies and blossom, taste the olive oil and wine, feel the cool of the shade and hear the voice of God calling to you in this garden. How does it feel to be surrounded by such an intensity of sense? What do you hear God saying to you? Spend as long as you can in the garden God has grown and know that he grows it for you.

You might like to contrast this with the emptiness of the wind storm of 8:7 and the barrenness that resulted there.

A psalm of resurrection

Your faithfulness ends in resurrection
Your truth turns to life
Your love has conquered death
Your tenderness brings new growth
Your promises last forever

So
I praise you in my joy.

Lord God, I know you understand what it is to be filled with joy; your resurrection proclaims that you do. You offer me life in all its fullness—all this I believe. May I live today and tomorrow knowing it is true.

When God speaks

Sally Welch

God's declaration of power

Imaginative

Read Psalm 50.

These readings explore the occasions in the Bible when God's voice is heard speaking to individuals. Through God's words to others we learn wisdom for our own lives.

Imagine the scene. It is 5.30 in the morning, by the shores of the Sea of Galilee. All is quiet, but it is not completely dark, for the dawn is approaching, and already the sky is lightening as the sun nears the horizon. There is no sound at the edge of the lake, only the rhythmic lapping of the waves on the shore as they gently break against the damp pebbles and small rocks which cluster there. At the eastern point of the lake, where two mountains descend towards each other, forming a deep valley, the sky is beginning to turn an orangey pink. Then, with a surprising speed, the first curve of light shows above the horizon, which is made even blacker in contrast. Silent but steady, the golden disc rises above the hills, sending out rays of colour across the grey sky in which the stars are already dimming. The light plays on the water of the lake, making it dance and sparkle, and in the distance birds begin their morning chorus. A crane flies low across the waves, its long neck tucked in, beak extended, blue legs forming an arrow-like shape, swift and silent, seeming to bring with it the full glory of the dawn. God has spoken. Listen to his voice.

Are there times when God has spoken to you using a language which is other than words? Have your heard God's voice in a beautiful landscape, or in the sound of birdsong or the laughter of a child? Recall that time and listen again to his voice. Today be attentive to his voice, striving to hear it even where you least expect it, and pause to listen to him.

'I must turn aside and look'

Spotlight

Read Exodus 3:1–8.

There are a great many references to mindfulness in our media and our daily lives at the moment; it is seen as a way of dealing with the challenges and stresses of everyday life, by not allowing ourselves to become consumed by them and so being able to manage them. The essence of mindfulness lies in practising the skill of 'waking up' to the present, of being aware of the present and focused in it. It means having a controlled, focused awareness of the entire contents of our consciousness, bodily movements, emotions, intentions and thoughts, including our own positive and negative reactions to these things. By separating out our awareness of all these things, we can respond intelligently to them, rather than allowing ourselves to be carried away by our emotions and desires. We can achieve this by focusing on the immediate moment, which is outwardly the ultimate in insignificance, but which cumulatively is the sum of all creation. This paradox, it seems to me, is linked to the paradox of our faith, the incarnate and transcendent God—the God who can be found in every tiny detail, who abides within us, and the God who is the creator of the universe, whose hands 'flung stars into space'. In this passage, God speaks to Moses and declares his nature, his very essence, in its grandness and in its compassion, and he sets before Moses his plan for saving the children of Israel. But before God can speak, Moses has first to be prepared to notice, to pause, to step outside his preoccupations and his inner monologue and see the miracles of creation that lie all around him.

Had Moses not 'turned aside' in wonder, he would not have allowed God the space to speak. How can we make space for God to speak to us today? Find a comfortable place to sit or lie—if this is not possible, find somewhere you can stand undisturbed for a short time. Make sure you feel supported and balanced in your body, relaxed but alert. Close your eyes if this helps. Focus your mind on your breath, feeling it enter and leave your body, filling your body with life. Picture yourself standing in Moses' place before the burning bush, and be silent before God, listening for his voice.

Rehydration

Creative

Read Ezekiel 37:1–14.

This famous passage from Ezekiel takes us to the valley of the dry bones, where death lies all around and there is no hope. God speaks to Ezekiel of his love for his people and promises them new life and the knowledge of God. There are occasions when we too feel as if we are in a spiritual desert, surrounded by the bones of our usual prayer practices which fail to sustain us in our dry times. Then we must listen for God's voice, reassuring us that if we keep faith our thirst will be quenched with his living water: 'And you shall live; and you shall know that I am the Lord' (Ezekiel 37:6).

For this exercise you will need a shallow bowl of water, a piece of paper, some scissors and a pencil.

On the paper, draw a flower (the bloom only, not the stalk or leaves) with five or seven large petals that do not overlap, so they can be folded down individually. Cut out your flower. Write in the centre of the flower any verses from Ezekiel 37 that speak to you ('I will put my spirit within you, and you shall live' (v. 14), for example). You can colour the petals with crayons if you wish. When you have done this, carefully fold the petals over the central part of the blossom. The petals will overlap each other.

Float the paper flower gently on the surface of the bowl of water. Notice how the petals slowly unfold to reveal the promises of God that you have written inside.

Eternal God and Father, help us to entrust the past to your mercy, the present to your love, and the future to your mercy, in the name of Jesus Christ, who is the same yesterday, today and for ever. Amen (source unknown).

'Where are you?'

Bible reading

Read Genesis 3:8.

This is possibly the most poignant section of the whole terrible story of Adam and Eve, that tale of the first act of disobedience and defiance and its disastrous consequences for the whole of humankind. God is fully aware of the fact that Adam and Eve have eaten some of the fruit of the tree of the knowledge of good and evil, despite having been warned not to. Admittedly they did so under provocation—first Eve, then Adam were beguiled and cajoled into taking the fruit and eating it—but the fact is that they did eat it, fully aware that to do so was to go against the wishes of their loving creator. Consider the deep disappointment with which God must have been filled, the consuming sadness at the knowledge of their choice, and his regret at the nature of the course of action which he must now take. But what we hear from God is not anger or hurt, not a call for punishment or vengeance, but a deeply loving appeal to the two miscreants to come from their hiding place and engage in dialogue with him. God calls to Adam and Eve to come into his presence, as he has called to his children for thousands of years, and as he still calls. Yes, Adam and Eve must face the consequences of their disobedience, but they will not face them alone, for God will always accompany them and will seek them and their children continually. Whatever we do, however far away from God we stray, we have but to stop and listen and we will hear his voice lovingly calling us and, as he seeks us, so the sound of his voice will guide us into his presence.

When you pray today, begin your prayers with your hands clenched into fists. Picture within those fists all the ugly things you have said and done that you would like to hide from God and from yourself. Gradually, open your hands so that they lie relaxed with palms upward. Offer to God your whole self, confident that he will transform everything in the light of his love.

'What are you doing here, Elijah?'

Spotlight

Read 1 Kings 19:9–12.

Elijah is exhausted and distraught. After all he has done in the name of the Lord, his faithful declarations on God's behalf, it seems as if all has been in vain and now his very life is in danger. Even in the depths of his terror and despair, however, Elijah does not turn away from God, but instead stands before him to find an answer. God's response to this angry, desperate man, who challenges the way God has directed events, is one of extreme gentleness. He encourages Elijah to pour out his anger and despair and listens with patience and love. Then he shows Elijah where indeed God is to be found—not in the noise and tumult, but in the silence.

Seeking God in silence has been a mainstay of Christian prayer throughout the centuries. It is only by ceasing to make noise ourselves that we will be able to hear the still, small voice of God. This noise might be the external noise of busy, preoccupied lives or the internal sounds of the constant running commentary we make upon our lives, insistently criticising or re-evaluating our words and actions. As you pray, be intentional in your seeking, deliberately making time to be still, both externally and internally, clearing a space in your diary and in your heart and mind to listen for the voice of God. At first this may be difficult, as your busy mind allows thoughts to distract you from your task, but you will improve with practice. You may find it helpful to repeat a simple prayer to help your concentration, gently turning from any selfish preoccupations towards God. With Teresa of Avila and with so many thousands of others, 'Let God's presence settle into your bones, and allow your soul the freedom to sing, dance, praise and love.'

God's teaching

Bible reading

Read Jonah 4:8–10.

There can be no doubt that righteous anger can be a powerful force. It was righteous anger that provoked Jesus to overturn the tables of the moneylenders in the temple; it was righteous anger that encouraged William Wilberforce to battle against slavery in the 19th century and righteous anger that led Martin Luther King to march against apartheid. However, Jonah's anger is not that of the righteous man, but of the self-righteous, and this is a vital difference.

Jonah has tried, out of fear, to avoid God's commission for him: to preach repentance to the people of Nineveh. Discovering after considerable hardship that God's call can only be postponed, but never escaped, he does finally make his way to Nineveh and give the people God's message, to which the Ninevites respond wholeheartedly, full of remorse, and promising to mend their ways, whereupon they are saved from destruction. But Jonah is deeply aggrieved that God's grace should be lavished on such undeserving people. Jonah's anger endangers his role—an angry, unbalanced prophet cannot be the effective mouthpiece of God; he must not allow his own frailties to corrupt God's will, and God must address this. He does so by means of a living metaphor, lovingly admonishing his fervent but misguided prophet.

We too must have the courage to stand up for what we believe is right, working for peace and justice wherever that takes us. However, like Jonah, we must also take care that we do not mistake righteous anger for the self-righteous stance of one who secretly believes they are better than their neighbours. Instead, open to God's will, we must be prepared to love our neighbours whatever the personal cost, while striving to bring God's kingdom ever closer.

'I have set my bow in the clouds'

Creative

Read Genesis 9:1–17.

The story of Noah is one of catastrophe and rescue, of sin and forgiveness, of the endless mercy of God. Noah's obedience is the direct cause of God's promise to his children that never again will the world suffer such total destruction. A covenant is made between God and the earth and, as stewards of this covenant, we must notice and hold fast to every sign of God's promise. Although we have spoiled much, great beauty surrounds us still. We can keep our part of the covenant by noticing and cherishing that beauty.

For this exercise you will need a large piece of paper and some crayons.

'Mindful colouring' has been found to help calm the mind and focus the concentration. Draw a rainbow on your paper, or find a rainbow pattern online and print it out. Carefully colour it in using the correct shades, reflecting as you do on the created world that surrounds you with its rainbow colours. Try to picture animals, insects, trees, plants and fish that are the colour you are using as you work your way through the spectrum. When you have finished, hang your rainbow where you can see it during the day.

The Promised Land

Spotlight

Read Genesis 17:8–9.

This is perhaps one of the most famous occasions when God speaks directly to one of his children, and in this speech he makes a covenant with Abraham which will be reasserted, reaffirmed and remembered for thousands of years. It is the promise of place, that there will be somewhere which all of God's people will be able to call home, a place where they can find security and a sense of permanence, where they will no longer feel as if they are strangers and aliens in a foreign land, but be able to put down roots. In this homeland will be the opportunity to settle, to grow deep into the soil which will belong to them for ever, passing down through the generations to their children and their children's children. In return, the people of God will keep their side of the covenant and live in God's ways, worshipping him alone and following his instructions for a healthy, loving and God-centred community. Throughout the Old Testament, this promise shines like a golden thread, encouraging and leading individuals and communities towards the fulfilment of the covenant. There are times when they go astray, failing to keep their side of the agreement, and these times are full of hardship and suffering. These are times of exile from the promised land, occasions for repentance, change and growth; the transformation is then complete, as the reintegrated nation takes up a new role. And always, God's presence and promise is with his people.

For Christians, this promised land is Christ himself, the fulfilment of the covenant, the place wherein we can put down roots; he is our homeland, our security, from whence flows the peace and love that only he can give.

Inviting God's voice

Prayers

Use these prayers to help you explore the different ways in which God has spoken to you and to others.

Breathe through the heats of our desire
Thy coolness and thy balm;
Let sense be dumb, let flesh retire;
Speak through the earthquake, wind, and fire,
O still, small voice of calm! (John Greenleaf Whittier)

Give us the strength to speak out on behalf of those who have no voice: the poor, the sick, the vulnerable. Put words in our mouths and courage in our hearts so that we may speak boldly for righteousness sake.

'Speak, Lord, for your servant is listening' (1 Samuel 3:9).

Lord, we pray that during the busy times we may hear you calling to us. Let us not be turned aside from hearing your voice by the distraction of other, lesser voices, but let us always be focused on you. We ask for the grace to set aside the time to listen and the wisdom to act on what we hear.

'I thank you, Father, that you listen to me' (John 11:41).

Father God, we thank you that you listen to us. Help us to wait patiently for your answers in faith, confident in your loving purposes for us.

We should listen to God

Imaginative

Read Psalm 95:6–8.

We stood at the crossroads, gazing anxiously at the map. This was a significant junction; a wrong turning now would take us many miles from that day's destination. We were tired, as we had been walking for many days—we could not physically afford a detour. Around us the chatter and bustle of the lively market town continued, incomprehensible to us as we spoke no Spanish. After days on the road the conversations and discussions of the inhabitants of villages and towns had become merely background noise, part of the environment through which we were travelling, easily ignored.

Our small son tugged anxiously at my trouser legs. Focused on route finding, I allowed this to continue for some time before turning somewhat irritably to discover what was wrong with him. He did not speak but simply waved his hand round the market square. All around us were people shouting and waving, pointing out the way we should go. Women leaned from upper windows, taxi drivers flapped their hands, grinning young men made signposts out of their bodies. Used to confused pilgrims, we were clearly a familiar sight to them and they were keen to help. We walked on, full of gratitude towards our son, who alone had stopped and listened.

God is constantly calling us, willing us to stop and listen to him. Take time to pause and rest, delighting in the loving call of God, responding to his love with praise and worship. Do not allow yourself, amidst the noise and confusion of daily life, to filter out the still small voice of love which beckons us ever onward in the one true direction. During the day, try to find somewhere to be still and listen for God's voice in the silence. If possible, have such a place available throughout your day, whether at work or in the home. It does not need to be large or particularly special; simply somewhere you can retreat for a while, to stop and listen.

'Ask what I should give you'

Bible reading

Read 1 Kings 3:4–9.

Many people today speculate on what they would do if they won the lottery. How to divide up the money, how much to give to charity or relatives, what to spend, what to save, is a topic of conversation that is guaranteed to provoke lively discussion, and to reveal much about the nature of the participants. How must Solomon have felt, when God spoke to him and asked him what he wanted? What must it have been like to have the entire world placed at your feet, the opportunity for limitless wealth and power displayed before you? Solomon would be forgiven for feeling dazzled and confused, but he shows neither of these emotions. Instead he calmly considers what gifts he will most need in order to carry out his responsibilities most effectively. He reflects on the ways in which he may best serve the people over whom he has been placed as ruler. He dismisses the glittering promises of wealth and power and instead asks for 'an understanding mind to govern your people, able to discern between good and evil'. What a humbling response this is to those of us who like to spend much time deliberating between a large house and a fast car, even the choice between giving to our favourite cause or to an impecunious relative. Hints of another man, also offered endless power and wealth, who rejected both in favour of walking closely with God, even though that walk would lead to his death on the cross, can make us more determined to listen to the true voice of God that speaks to us from the wilderness of material greed and earthly power. What gifts do you ask for from God today? What do you need to serve him now?

'This is my Son'

Imaginative

Read Matthew 3:1–17.

Imagine the scene. There is a huge crowd standing by the banks of the River Jordan. Some people are standing at quite a distance from the river, peering over the heads of others to see what is happening. Others line the river-banks, with a good view of what is going on in the water, reserving the option to join in, but held back by doubt as to what it all really means. Still others stumble down the uneven slopes and join John, the son of Zechariah, in the cold, rushing heart of the river where they are thrust down into its murky depths before being pulled up, spluttering and gasping with the shock. John's stentorian voice can be heard across the landscape as he urges the crowd to repent of their sins. He cuts a strange figure, wearing nothing but a sodden animal skin wrapped around his loins, his body lean and sinewy from his harsh living conditions. But the power of his faith is compelling and more and more join him in the water, confessing their sins so they can be washed clean.

A strange silence falls upon the crowd as a figure moves slowly amongst it. It is Jesus, walking by himself. He descends the river-bank, now slippery with mud, and approaches John, wading carefully through the water. But John's eagerness has vanished and there is a new hesitancy in his gestures. He shakes his head at Jesus' words, which are too quiet for the crowd to hear. Slowly, Jesus sinks into the water. Slowly, John retrieves him from beneath the river's turbulent surface. As Jesus' head breaks through into the air once again, a voice is heard: 'This is my Son, the Beloved, with whom I am well pleased.'

Now there can be no room for doubt, for the task has begun.

Watching and waiting

Susan Blagden

Waiting

Introduction/imaginative

As Advent dawns once again, we consider how we might watch and wait as the world, and even the Church sometimes, rushes more and more frantically towards Christmas.

We will take time to consider what we wait for, how we wait, and most importantly why we wait, drawing on the scriptures and other writers, poets and musicians, as we learn about 'watching and waiting'.

As we begin, I invite you to take some time and jot down the places in which you often find yourself waiting in the course of ordinary day-to-day life. Perhaps the times we wait most are when we travel. In the winter we may need to wait for the car to warm up so we can clear the windscreen. We wait for traffic lights to tell us it is safe to continue on our journey. We wait for trains, behind a yellow safety line, and we wait in departure lounges for aeroplanes to take us to different cultures and time zones. Jot down also what you are waiting for in each place.

This first week of Advent is when we traditionally remember our forebears in faith. Abraham and Sarah are some of the earliest who have something to teach us about waiting. In Genesis 18:1–15 God makes a promise to Abraham that he will have a son and that his descendants will be more than the grains of sand on the seashore. This seems a rather far-fetched idea. Sarah laughs at the improbability of it all. Humanly speaking it *was* preposterous. But then God *had* promised.

Using the story in Genesis 18, imagine yourself like Abraham at home, being interrupted in your tasks to welcome unexpected visitors with an unexpected message. Let the story unfold for you. How do you respond? How is God asking you to wait? How are you to spend this waiting time? What does it feel like? Ask God for whatever grace you need for this waiting time.

Conclude your prayer time by using this verse, changing Abraham's name for your own.

'[Abraham] considered him faithful who had promised' (Hebrews 11:11).

Waiting and preparation...

Prayer

'Keep awake therefore, for you know neither the day nor the hour' (Matthew 25:13).

Waiting is strongly linked with promise. It anticipates something being different. We wait because we have been promised a gift, or a visit by someone we know and love or wish to meet. In anticipation of this we stay in the place where we are likely to receive the gift and/or meet the person.

Jesus' story about five wise and five foolish bridesmaids helps us in our waiting. Prayerfully and slowly read the words in Matthew 25:1–13. The wise bridesmaids had anticipated a long wait. The foolish ones did not take time to anticipate what they needed. In the end their lack of preparation meant they were shut out of the bridegroom's presence. A shut door is a powerful metaphor.

Use the simple invocation: 'Maranatha—Come, Lord Jesus, come.'

Repeat this prayer for five or ten minutes, becoming aware of the connection between the promised return of Christ in glory and a deepening desire within you to be ready. This will have a practical working out in your daily life. What do you need to do to be expectant and prepared? As you consider the closed door, the night, the oil and the light, what resources do you need to wait for the Lord's return? Talk to the Lord about any blocks to being prepared that you sense within yourself.

Who is waiting with you? How will you help and encourage each other through the dark hours of not knowing the time of our Lord's return? What does it feel like to be ready and welcomed or not ready and excluded?

This is a simple prayer that you can return to at any time during the busyness of the day or the solitude of the night. You might also return to it when you are forced to wait and perhaps resent the waiting time. This is one way of turning frustration to good effect!

Watching and waiting with hope

Prayer/intercession

'Now hope that is seen is not hope. For who hopes for what is seen? But if we hope for what we do not see, we wait for it with patience' (Romans 8: 24–25).

Advent reminds us that we are expecting the return of Jesus and the final fulfilment of the kingdom of God. The world has carried on for 2000 plus years since Jesus foretold his return. Therefore, we may be tempted to join Sarah in laughing at the improbability of God's promise. And yet…?

The last verse of Charles Wesley's rousing Advent hymn: 'Lo, he comes with clouds descending' reminds us of that promise:

Yea, amen, let all adore thee,
High on thine eternal throne;
Saviour, take the power and glory,
Claim the kingdom for thine own;
Alleluia!
Thou shalt reign, and thou alone.

Spend time in prayer with these words and use these three simple steps:

Adoration: write or sing your prayers of adoration as you give thanks for the steadfastness of God's love for you.

Affirmation: that the kingdom is God's. Bring the events from today's news into your prayer with words or pictures from the newspaper. Notice in the news the different kingdoms of the world and in your prayer ask for God's kingdom to come in all its power and glory.

Alleluia: praise rings out when we know we are totally aligned with what God asks. Ask God through the Holy Spirit to show you any areas of your life where he is not yet reigning supreme. Also ask God to show you what to do in prayer, or in practical involvement in politics or issues of social justice, to help God's kingdom become more of a reality on earth.

We live in the here and now and our spirits are focused on the future. We watch and wait in prayer because we have this hope within us, that God's kingdom will finally be established. We wait for this with patience because, as Hebrews 10:23 reminds us, 'he who has promised is faithful'.

Prophets wait for the Lord

Going out

One of the many Old Testament references to waiting for the Lord that has stayed with me to underpin my priestly ministry is Habakkuk 2:1: 'I will stand at my watch-post and station myself on the rampart; I will keep watch to see what he will say to me, and what he will answer concerning my complaint.'

Habakkuk's complaint was about the amount of evil in the world. It seemed as if God was inactive. Yet Habakkuk remained at his post. He stationed himself on the rampart—a place that was a fortress, a place that was raised up, a place where he could see far and wide.

Notice that word, 'stand'. The physical posture matters. We stand as a sign of attentiveness, of readiness to move. We stand with every fibre of our being on high alert, watching.

The purpose of prayer, particularly Advent prayer, is to watch. Like Habakkuk, we may see much that is evil and we may feel overwhelmed by it all. However, as we stand in our place of prayer whilst seeing the evil in our world, we need to attune our heart's eye to the Lord in his holy temple (Habakkuk 2:20).

We wait with a focus on the Lord. Habakkuk sees God in the temple. Worship is at the heart of waiting.

Where is your equivalent of Habakkuk's rampart? If you live in a walled city you could spend your prayer time walking the walls or stationed on its ramparts. If you live near the coast you might find a watchtower or a cliff that helps you to pray from a rampart-like place.

If you are able, spend your prayer time standing. Notice how it helps or hinders your praying and your sense of attentiveness in waiting for God to respond to you.

In your equivalent of Habakkuk's rampart see how the place as well as the posture of prayer help you to wait in the midst of so much that is unholy.

Zechariah—waiting in silence

Reflective

Read Luke 1:5–24.

In Advent we also focus on John the Baptist, the forerunner of Jesus. Zechariah was a priest serving in the temple. He was visited by an angel and told that he and his wife Elizabeth, even in their old age, would have a son. Zechariah, with human wisdom, argued that this was impossible. The result was that he lost the power of speech for the entire duration of Elizabeth's pregnancy! Now Zechariah was a religious person, supposedly a man who believed in God and God's ability to do anything. As a priest, he must surely have known the story of Abraham and Sarah. Yet he doubted what God had said to him through the angel.

One of the gifts of Zechariah's story is to show us that, whatever our personality type, we all need to know how to shut up and really listen to what God says to us.

3D Coaching has a great coaching tip called WAIT—Why Am I Talking? The tip challenges us to remain silent unless we can improve the silence with our words!

Zechariah was forced to do this. Traditionally Advent has been a time of fasting, perhaps not as prominently as in Lent, but it is still a valid practice.

How might you fast from speech? It may not achieve anything to fast totally from speech like Zechariah, but it might help your spiritual life if you regularly ask: Why Am I Talking? Practise this at home, work or college. What difference does it make? Notice your feelings. You may want to find a way to confess your own areas of unbelief. One cautionary note: this shouldn't be used to prove how disciplined you are (or not!); rather, it is a chance intentionally to refrain from chattering in order that you might become more attuned to the voice of God.

Mary waiting expectantly

Creative

Read Luke 1:46–55.

Now we turn our attention to Mary, the mother of our Lord. Despite a great deal of speculation about the circumstances in which the annunciation took place, very little is actually known. We don't know whether Mary was watching or waiting for God. What we do know is that she was attuned enough to recognise this as a 'God moment' even if unlooked for and unasked. Maybe it was too obvious for her to have missed, or maybe she noticed it because she was practised at watching and waiting. Either way, Luke records her response to this unexpected gift in the words of the Magnificat—Mary's song of praise. As Mary begins this waiting time, her focus is not on herself but on God and what he will bring about through this gift. It is a song of confidence as she looks to the future.

Philip Doddridge's 18th-century Advent hymn enjoins each one of us:

> Hark the glad sound! The Saviour comes,
> The Saviour promised long;
> Let every heart prepare a throne,
> And every voice a song.

Write your own song of praise or express it visually. Seek to weave together the same themes as the Magnificat. Try praying the Magnificat, or a phrase of it each day, letting it sink into the depths of your being. Consciously experience how waiting with this sense of hope and confidence affects your daily life and engagement with the world.

Watching and waiting for the return of the king

Intercession

Read Matthew 25:31–46.

'When the Son of Man comes in his glory, and all the angels with him, then he will sit on the throne of his glory' (Matthew 25:31).

Jesus promised he would return to this earth. In this passage from Matthew, just as the angels sang of the glory of God at Jesus' first coming, so they wait to direct glory again to the king when he finally returns to claim the kingdom for his own. It may seem as if Christendom has waited an inordinately long time for Jesus to come back. We need to be careful that this doesn't cause us to be cynical about it ever happening.

'Your kingdom come' we pray in the Lord's Prayer. How often do we realise that in making that request, we are meant to provide at least part of the answer? Matthew reminds us of core kingdom values of recognising Christ in the other and helping those in need. Social justice is a core value of Christian faith and is referenced strongly in many Advent hymns.

The hymn writers draw their inspiration from the Old Testament prophets who frequently directed people to be attentive to these issues. Perhaps none put it more succinctly than Micah (6:8):

'What does the Lord require of you but to do justice, and to love kindness, and to walk humbly with your God?' We have no choice but to engage with these issues.

What are we waiting for? We are waiting for a world where there is fairness and justice, where those who have readily share with those who have not. We do this because we believe in God's plenteous provision and faithfulness.

Take some news items regarding justice issues into prayer, perhaps singing your prayers using some of the Advent hymns. Decide what you can do this Advent to help others, remembering, of course, that there are a lot of fairly traded Christmas cards and gifts available; choosing to buy such things helps to establish something more of God's kingdom here on earth.

Mary waiting in hiddenness

Imaginative

'Whenever you pray, go into your room and shut the door and pray to your Father who is in secret; and your Father who sees in secret will reward you' (Matthew 6:6).

Whatever the circumstances were of the annunciation, we do know that Mary didn't have the benefit of today's technology and would not have seen her child in utero! The growth took place, as it always does, in the darkness, out of sight.

Sieger Koder, a contemporary artist, has produced a thoughtful image called *Mary*. In it Mary's hands are open, but her eyes are closed. She appears to be kneeling. Above her is depicted the Christ-child developing in her womb and both of them are enfolded or overshadowed by God. It reminds us that this slow work of human growth takes place in the darkness. We cannot speed it up. It will take its own time.

Increasingly today we live our lives in public view far more than any previous generation. However, we must choose how to nurture this secret life of God within us even though we can't see it. Jesus invites us to do this by spending time in hiddenness, praying to our Father. Intimate relationships need protected time and attention. It is no different with God.

You are invited to have a physical hidden place of prayer or simply an awareness of that secret place being within you. Imagine a shut door—this time you are on the right side of it—behind which you can nurture your relationship with God. What do you need in order to do this? In prayer express to God your desires or fears about being totally enfolded in love. Talk with God about your own prayer times and where you have them. What do they feel like? Are they are simply a duty or are they an expression of a real sense of attentive waiting on God? You may find it helpful to download a copy of Koder's image to help your prayers. Take time to rest in God's presence.

Mary waiting with Elizabeth

Imaginative/reflective

Read Luke 1:39–45.

This story gives us a strong visual representation of the meeting between Mary and Elizabeth, along with John and Jesus leaping in their mothers' wombs. In her waiting time, Mary needed the wisdom and companionship of her older relative, Elizabeth. We all need someone to walk with us on our journey of faith. This story says much about how we wait with another—encircled but not stifled—with closeness and yet with spaciousness for the movement of the Holy Spirit, nurturing new life in the space between. I find this to be a helpful illustration of the ministry of spiritual direction or having a soul friend. The ministry is primarily about helping us to discern the movement of the Holy Spirit in a person's life. It is a place of vulnerability, honesty, loving challenge and real growth.

Take some time to reflect on and give thanks for the wise people in your life. For whom are you also a wise person, a companion on the journey? What might this story have to say about the way you relate to each other, and the place of the Holy Spirit as the ultimate soul friend?

In prayer imagine yourself as one or other of the characters in this Bible passage. Let the story unfold. What do you say to each other? How do you tell your story of God's action in your life? What is it that you most want to share? What is it like to hear the other's story of the Holy Spirit's activity? What is God inviting you to discover or experience as you draw alongside each other as companions on the way? Conclude your time by giving thanks for the gifts.

Simeon and Anna

Prayer

Read Luke 2: 25–38.

Although the story of Simeon and Anna properly belongs to the Feast of the Presentation (Candlemas), their examples are key in understanding the theme of watching and waiting that is our focus during Advent.

Here we have two older people—a priest in the temple looking for 'the consolation of Israel' and a widow who has committed herself to prayer and fasting for 'the redemption of Jerusalem'. We see here the faithfulness of watching and waiting in prayer over many years. They were praying for a nation (Israel) as well as praying for a place (Jerusalem). We do not know the content of their prayers but we do know that their faithfulness in watching and waiting enabled them to be in the right place at the right time, and to recognise God's presence finally in their midst.

The fruit of that kind of faithfulness, over so many years, brought an ability to speak clearly and directly. Simeon spoke words of truth into the heart of the lives of Mary and Joseph. This kind of prayer means that we are continually refined and cleared of clutter, able to be a clear channel for words of challenge and also words of blessing to those people who cross our path in the waiting time. We become increasingly able to recognise *kairos*—God's time. This helps us to wait with expectation and hope.

Take time to write prayers of blessing for people, situations, places, world events and world leaders. Practise praying prayers of blessings on all those who interrupt your day or come into your waiting space. Give thanks for the blessings you have received. What difference does it makes to your day when you pray prayers of blessing on those who come into your 'waiting' space?

Waiting—the gaze of love

Prayer

'Behold, I am the handmaid of the Lord, let it be to me according to your word' (Luke 1:38).

'Behold!' is an imperative that used to appear frequently in our Bible translations. More recent versions have reduced it to the simple invitation 'Look'. In reality there is a world of difference between these two little words. In today's busy world a brief scan often suffices for quickly absorbing information. It is easy to look briefly. 'Behold' commands the viewer to pause and to give time and attention to that which needs to be seen. Once again we find Mary to be our inspiration for living this out. Note how she is able to respond to the action of God's spirit in her life by saying 'Behold, I am the handmaid of the Lord, let it be to me according to your word.' Implicit in the word 'behold' is a sense of relationship. Mary affirms in her Magnificat that God has looked with favour upon her. Mary responds to that affirming look by asking God to look upon her. There is something transformative about the gaze of God in our lives. It changes how we see ourselves and how we understand our relationship to God. Mary is clear that she is now a handmaid. This is not a menial response but a willing and joyful response of love to love. There is always a servant heart as a core dynamic of any genuine love. A handmaid waits because she is looking to her mistress in order to see how best she can serve. Attention is closely allied to intention.

Take time in prayer to wait and gaze on God and to let him gaze on you. This is wordless prayer and may not feel comfortable. Notice your emotions and talk with God as appropriate about what you feel, whether that's joy and a deep sense of love or whether you find it difficult and would rather not do this! Tears may well up and if they do, just let them. They can be healing and enable a deeper intimacy. Mary was very in touch with her intention to be totally attentive to God's call in her life. 'Handmaid' may not be your metaphor. If not, what does work for you?

The meaning is in the waiting

Reflective

Read Ephesians 1:17–18.

As we noted at the beginning, we often wait because we expect someone or something. We wait because we have an end in mind. This gives purpose to our waiting. R.S. Thomas in his poem, 'Kneeling', rather challenges that idea! We so often wait in prayer because we are waiting for God's guidance to us, or for God to speak to us through the scriptures. We wait because we expect God to give us something. R.S. Thomas' experience was that when we begin to speak about what we have received, we have immediately also lost something. Waiting is a valid experience in its own right. It does not have to mean that we are waiting for an outcome. Rather there is a sense that waiting is very much an active state of being. As the gift of God grows within us, we, like Mary, find ourselves changed, stretched and challenged. Every fibre of our being is involved in this new life. We wait, often with an increasingly heightened sense of awareness. We grow into the likeness of Christ, at least in part, by actively and attentively watching and waiting.

Take some time in prayer to ask God to help you to be more focused in your prayer and to be released from the need always to expect something to happen. Commit yourself to practical ways of living more intentionally to help establish God's kingdom. What do you need to do to continue to strengthen the skills of watching and waiting in prayer? Commit yourself to this way of prayerful living for a set period of time; for example, a week or a month or through to Candlemas (2 February).

Maranatha! Come, Lord Jesus.

Gifts

Sally Smith

Gifts

Introduction/creative

For many people presents are the most important part of Christmas; hours are spent in deciding on the right gift, and the expense mounts up. At this time of the year our televisions and letter boxes tell us what we should be buying for whom and raising our expectations of what we might find under the tree on Christmas Day. Hours are spent wrapping presents so they each look beautiful.

So, how can we find Jesus in the gifts we offer and receive? What are the gifts he wants to give you this Christmas? And are you ready to receive what he has to offer?

I invite you to begin by creating a gift from God. Choose an empty box. Look through your wrapping paper and ribbons and choose the ones you would like him to use to wrap your present. Sit down in a quiet place with plenty of time and space, and wrap your box. As you do so, acknowledge that this is a gift from God that you are wrapping. Allow him to wrap it with you. Take extra care over how you wrap the present; be slow and deliberate in your actions. Add ribbons and bows as seems appropriate for such an important present.

As you wrap, notice how it feels. Recognise and stay with the feelings you have and share them with God.

Choose or make a gift tag to go with your present. What does God want to say to you on the tag? Receive his words as you receive his gift.

When the present is ready, hold it carefully, receive it and acknowledge the giver of the gift.

Keep it somewhere where it will remind you of God's gift to you and of his desires for you this Christmas.

There will be suggestions in these notes of how to use this gift to help you pray as we head towards Christmas. You may find it becomes a present to and from different people; allow it to change as it needs to.

Gifts to Jesus

Creative

Gifts are given to the parents of any new baby. There may be practical gifts to help them through those first few difficult weeks, helping them to set up all the things needed to look after a baby well; there may be gifts with symbolism to inspire or support the parents over the coming months and years or there may be gifts for the baby in later life. We are reminded every year that when Jesus was born he was given gifts of gold, frankincense and myrrh, which we interpret to be gifts of symbolism for his life ahead. As with any newborn baby, that was not all he was given. Traditionally we think of the shepherds as bringing a lamb as a gift. The innkeeper gave hospitality—the only space he had available he gave. I imagine that his wife, once she knew of the birth, would have been out into the stable with blankets and food, or with the advice of someone who was already a mother to a young girl without her own mother.

Allow your imagination to get to work and let it be fanciful if it goes that way. Who else would have been around in Bethlehem and what gifts might they have brought to Mary, Joseph and Jesus? They may be practical or symbolic, they may just be sharing in the excitement of the event of new birth (you might imagine the innkeeper giving Joseph a drink to wet the baby's head!). Remember all that Mary and Joseph were able to give (a loving family, faith in his heavenly father, security and protection). Don't stick to fact, but be inspired by the events.

You could write a list of all the gifts that were given at that birth, or draw a simple stable and add words or pictures of the gifts, filling the space with the gifts given to Jesus and his parents in those first few days. If you have a nativity scene, you could write or draw the gifts on small cards and put them into the scene.

Give thanks for all those who were there at that amazing time to support and who (paraphrasing Christina Rossetti in the carol 'In the bleak mid-winter') were able to do their part.

Leave your gift at the altar

Reflective

Read Matthew 5:23–24.

Christmas is a time when we often notice the broken relationships we've been living with or avoiding during the rest of the year. As we write our cards one may be harder to write than the others or we may find we write some with an attitude of reluctance or anger. If you haven't already written your cards, as you do so, notice any names that seem harder to write than others, if there are any people on the list to whom you hesitate to send a card this year, or any names that are missing from the list. If you have already written your cards, pause and remember when you wrote them. You might want to look at your list and read the names there and be aware of any feelings some names may invoke, and cards that were harder to write than others or which you didn't write in the end. As you receive cards, notice how each one makes you feel.

Hold your present. As you hold it, think of one of the people for whom it was harder to write a card. What do you need to do to make things right with that person? It might be that you can only make the first step, but what would that first step be? It might be a note to add in the card, or something to say as you give it to them.

Now might be the time to do what needs to be done to mend the relationship between you, or it might be the time to stand before God with the gift you want to give to them and ask for his presence with you and with that other person. Leave the present before God while you go and do what needs to be done.

When you return to the present, tell God what has happened and thank him for his forgiveness and for his strength in helping you to mend broken relationships.

What I can I give him

Imaginative

Read Mark 12:41–44.
Imagine the scene: you are standing in the temple with Jesus and some of the disciples, close to the large bowls used to collect offerings from people. Look around and see the people near you. Listen to the noises of the temple.

Watch as people dressed in rich clothing come up and make their offerings. Listen as their large coins land in the bowls. Hear the quality of the sound they make.

You notice a widow, possibly an older lady, slowly coming towards the bowls. From her dress you guess that she does not have much money to spare. Watch as she comes closer and puts two small copper coins into the bowl. Listen to the different noise they make. Watch as she quietly walks away.

Then you notice Jesus calling you and the disciples over to

him. He says, 'The truth is that this poor widow gave more to the collection than all the others put together. All the others gave what they'll never miss; she gave extravagantly what she couldn't afford—she gave her all' (*THE MESSAGE*). Watch her disappear into the crowd, the woman who gave her all.

Turn to Jesus. What do you want to say to him? What does he want to say to you? Allow the conversation to continue. You may want to offer the gift to Jesus. What does it represent? What are you giving to him? Return to the words of the carol: 'What I can I give him—give my heart.'

What Jesus gave up for us

Imaginative/creative

When babies are born they don't bring physical gifts, but they do bring a great deal into the lives of those around them. Like any other baby, Jesus would have brought immense joy and delight and love. He would have changed the lives of Mary and Joseph as every baby changes the lives of their parents. As the son of God he brought other things as well. He would have brought anxiety over the task of raising not just a baby, but the son of God and all that Mary knew, or was beginning to imagine, would happen to him.

Spend some time imagining what Jesus would have brought into the lives of those around him. Again, you could list them or draw them, or add them to your nativity scene, filling the space with the gifts that were around at the time.

But Jesus, as well as giving a great deal, gave up a great deal. If you can, find the words of the carol 'Thou who wast rich beyond all splendour'. This was written in China in the early 20th century at a time when Christian missionaries were being captured and beheaded in that country. It was inspired by 2 Corinthians 8:9: 'For you know the generous act of our Lord Jesus Christ, that though he was rich, yet for your sakes he became poor, so that by his poverty you might become rich.' Spend some time thinking of the things Jesus would have given up when he became a man. The carol talks about the physical riches and environment, the praise and worship that he gave up because of his love for us. You could create a separate list for these, or place them outside the nativity scene, symbolising the things he left behind, that he gave up, when he was born. You might want to add your 'present' to the scene. Where do you place it? Is it something given to Jesus or something he gave up for you?

Thank Jesus for the things he gave up for you.

Christ as gift

Reflective

How often do we hear that the greatest gift of Christmas is Christ himself? He was the gift to the world from God the Father. But what does that actually mean for you? What exactly is the gift the Father gives us when he allows Christ to be born on earth? He is certainly one of those amazing gifts that every parent must dream of for their children; he lasts forever; he changes over time so is always just right at the right time, and he challenges and consoles us. He is what we need at each moment.

He was given to the world as a baby, a precious vulnerable gift. He left earth crucified, killed because of humanity's wrongs. Hold your present and allow the different aspects of God's gift to the world to come into your thoughts, recalling the son that the Father gave to the world and all that means and has meant for you.

Read Mary's great song, the Magnificat (Luke 1:46–55), as a reminder of who she believed Jesus would be when she agreed to be his mother. You may want to try reading it in a different version from the one you usually use, as a fresh way of hearing well-known words. Which words from the song resonate with you today?

> *What God has done for me will never be forgotten,*
> *the God whose very name is holy, set apart from all others.*
> *His mercy flows in wave after wave*
> *on those who are in awe before him.*
> *He bared his arm and showed his strength,*
> *scattered the bluffing braggarts.*
>
> *He knocked tyrants off their high horses,*
> *pulled victims out of the mud.*
> *The starving poor sat down to a banquet;*
> *the callous rich were left out in the cold.*
> *He embraced his chosen child, Israel;*
> *he remembered and piled on the mercies, piled them high.*
>
> LUKE 1:46–54 *THE MESSAGE*

As you hold your present, receive the Christ who is being given for and to you now. Delight in the gift and then give thanks to the giver.

Gifts of the Spirit

Creative/Bible study

In the New Testament we read several times of the spiritual gifts given to the early churches for the building up of the body of the Church. They were given freely through God's grace.

Look at the following five passages and make five lists of the gifts that are mentioned in them. As you make the lists, notice the similarities and differences between them.

1 Corinthians 12:4–13
1 Corinthians 12:28–31
1 Corinthians 13:1–3
Romans 12:6–9
Ephesians 4:11–16

These gifts were not given so that the people who received them would be better people, or nicer to live with or so that they could be seen to do wonderful things. Paul says specifically that the gifts were given so that those who received them could better serve the body. We do not receive these gifts for our own benefit, but to enable God's work to be done and so that his people may grow. They are for the mutual need and benefit of the body.

Look again at your five lists. Which gifts do you feel you have been given?

If they are given for the building up of the body, then how are you using those gifts to do that? How are you using them to serve others in God's name?

This can be a hard question. We may have gifts we are not using at the moment, and we should not start using them because we feel guilty about not doing so. But it is good to consider what we have and how we might be being called to use those gifts for the body in which we live. Don't be hard on yourself if you have unused gifts, but do ask God why he gave them to you and if there is anything you should be doing with them now.

Which gifts from the lists do you think are needed in your church at the moment? Talk to God about them and about his work in your local area. Be ready to listen to him as well.

It is more blessed to give than to receive

Reflective

At the end of his sermon to the elders of the church at Ephesus Paul quotes Jesus: 'It is more blessed to give than to receive' (Acts 20:35). This saying is not recorded in the Gospels, but is likely to have been said by Jesus at some point. The context for this statement for Paul is that he is making his final speech to the elders; he has recalled some of the things he has endured and how he has supported himself and his companions and provided for those weaker than himself where possible.

The giving and receiving of gifts at Christmas is fraught with dangers—getting the wrong thing, spending too much or too little, receiving when you haven't given or giving when you don't receive... When we consider presents there needs to be both a giver and a receiver and there is the opportunity for each to be blessed. In the Bible we read about gifts both to God and from God, but there is also a recognition that gifts could be used as a bribe or to open doors (Proverbs 18:16). The New Testament places a strong emphasis on the gifts of God to individuals which are given freely. This may be salvation or eternal life, or the spiritual gifts. Salvation is the core gift that Jesus brought.

With each gift you give and receive this year, try pausing as you receive it. Accept it and before you open it enjoy the simple experience of receiving a gift. With each gift you give, again, pause and enjoy the experience of giving a gift away from the anxieties this can bring.

Thank God for the privilege of being able to give and receive gifts.

The shepherds brought gifts

Creative

The shepherds brought gifts that represented the everyday nature of their lives. They didn't have time to make anything or buy something special. They arrived at the stable with what they had to hand. It was these representations of their lives and their work that they offered to the baby Jesus.

Look around you. What do you see close to hand that you could offer to Jesus as representing your life and your work? Hold it and recall when you last used it, what you were doing and the impact that it had on you and on others.

Invite Jesus to be present as you remember how you have used this in the past. Then turn and offer it to him now. Watch his response as he receives it as a precious gift from you. With it offer all that it represents of your life and your work. How does it feel to offer that to God? Allow him to hold it.

Then receive it back from God. What does he say as he returns it to you? How does he want you to use it in the future? What does he say about its use in the past?

You could tie a ribbon round it or give it a gift tag, as a reminder that you gave this object and all it stands for to God. When you next use it, remember that you are sharing this with God.

Too many gifts

Intercession

By now, if you watch television, you will be fed up with the endless adverts telling you what you need in order to have a perfect Christmas. They will tell you what you have to give to your loved ones if they are to enjoy 25 December. What the adverts won't have done is remind you of the people who don't get any presents at Christmas, people who will not be able to go out and buy the perfect meal and presents that will make the day the most special ever.

As you watch the adverts, or look at the fliers and catalogues that come through your door over the next few days, look at the message they give you. Imagine the circumstances of people who see them, knowing that they could never afford to give or provide on this level, and hold those people before God.

Many aid organisations run Christmas campaigns. You may feel inspired to find out more about one and get involved.

All the presents

Reflective

As the pile of presents grows under the tree (or whatever the practice is in your house) spend some time praising God for all he has given you. On the other hand, it may be that your pile of presents is small and isn't growing. Thank him for those presents, and the people they represent, for the quality of those gifts and the people behind them. If the pile is huge, recognise God's abundance in giving, his ability to give to overflowing.

Christmas Eve is often known as the most holy of nights. It is the night when, at some point, Jesus became man. We don't know exactly when he was born. We go to bed and then we wake up in the morning and the world has changed overnight into a world in which Christ is present. It is a night of mystery and wonder. It is a night for waiting and watching to receive that most precious gift. As you pause, just before that night, remember Jesus' birth, his becoming Emmanuel, God with us. Remember that he is God. Experience the expectation of what that night will bring.

'How silently, how silently, the wondrous gift is given.'

As you prepare to receive Christ, you might like to light a candle and have some quiet waiting time. Hold your present and feel the anticipation of the receipt of the gift of light.

'The people who walked in darkness have seen a great light; those who lived in a land of deep darkness—on them light has shined' (Isaiah 9:2).

That was Christmas

Creative

Often, we get to a point on Christmas Day when we think, 'Well, that was Christmas.' There is that sense of anti-climax that sometimes comes. The presents have been unwrapped, the great meal eaten, and now what? When you reach this point, I suggest you return to your present and hold it again. Allow it to retell the story of what you have explored together. Receive again the gifts that have come with it and that you have given through it. Receive again the Christ who comes, not just in the spectacle of Christmas and the beautifully wrapped parcels, but the Christ who comes all year, who will stay with you for the rest of the year, long after you have tidied away the cards and eaten the last of the turkey.

Thank God for the gifts you have received and then, when you are ready, carefully unwrap your present, asking God what final gift might still be there beneath the paper. Be ready to receive one more present from him. Notice how you feel as you remove the ribbon and the paper and throw them away.

You might want to keep the gift tag for a while as a reminder of God's everlasting gifts to you.

Continuing to celebrate

Helen Julian CSF

Boxing Day

Introduction

Christmas trails so much baggage with it. By the time the day arrives we've all had weeks if not months of countdown, with increasingly frantic advertising, financial pressure, work parties, perhaps complicated family negotiations about who spends Christmas where and with whom, and finally turkey anxiety. Churchgoers can add in carol services, Christingles and nativity plays.

The temptation on 26 December is to heave a sigh of relief and try to forget all about it until next year. But the days between Christmas and New Year are for many people time off from work, and these days can be an opportunity gently to reflect on Christmas and all that it means. Officially the season lasts until 6 January (or even to 2 February) and there's a good reason for that; there's far too much to take in all at once. The Christmas stories are rich, rather like a large hamper; it takes time to unwrap all their contents, to appreciate them, and to make use of them.

So the invitation for this week is certainly to take a deep breath—but then to let it out and to relax into this time.

It might help to clear the decks as you start. Sit quietly somewhere where you won't be disturbed (tell the family firmly you're to be left in peace for a little while if you need to), and reflect on Christmas Day. Let your mind wander over all the details—who you were with, what you did, eating and drinking, celebrating, perhaps also remembering those who weren't with you and grieving for them.

What do you want to give thanks for?

What do you need to let go of?

What or who might you need to forgive?

If the festivities have left a trail of debris across the house you might find it helpful to do this as you clear up. Perhaps from this reflection you might identify something you want to reflect on in the coming week, or perhaps it will simply clear the way for things to emerge as the week goes on.

Encounter God with the shepherds

Bible reading

Read Luke 2:8–12, 15.

'In that region there were shepherds living in the fields, keeping watch over their flock by night. Then an angel of the Lord stood before them, and the glory of the Lord shone around them, and they were terrified' (Luke 2:8–9).

The shepherds have never been one of the more desirable roles in the nativity play. If you don't get the coveted role of Mary or Joseph, then the kings or the angels have better costumes and more glamour. In my time at least, the shepherds were traditionally kitted out in dressing gowns, with a headdress made of a tea towel.

And this reflects the reality of the life of a shepherd when Jesus was born. Shepherds couldn't keep the religious laws because of their work, and so were looked down on. They were the sort of men you didn't want your daughter to marry. And when they came into the village or town people might well suspect them of being up to no good.

Yet these are the first people to hear the news of Jesus' birth.

God, in the form of an angel, his messenger, comes to them out in the fields, as they huddle around their fire, to bring this stupendous news. It's not surprising that they were terrified. They didn't expect God to turn up at work, and mostly neither do we. Too easily we put God into a box, expecting communication in church or when we pray privately, but at 10.30 on a Tuesday morning?

What difference would it make if we did? How might it affect how we value the work we do (whether paid or unpaid) if God might turn up at any moment, bringing amazing news?

The shepherds may not have been able to be properly 'religious'—but they knew what to do when God spoke to them. They didn't sit around wondering what it all meant or whether they'd really experienced it. They got up and went to see for themselves. Their practical response could be something to aspire to in the new year.

Praise God with the angels

Creative

'And suddenly there was with the angel a multitude of the heavenly host, praising God and saying, "Glory to God in the highest heaven, and on earth peace among those whom he favours!" '(Luke 2:13–14).

Do you ever speculate what life in heaven will be like? I do—and one of the things I'm hoping for is to be able to sing beautifully (along with chocolate, cake and sticky toffee pudding having no calories, of course). But for now my voice is far from angelic.

However, I can still enjoy music as a way of praising God: joining in with a large congregation where my voice won't be heard, listening to favourite songs, singing in the shower or in the car, even letting my body respond to the rhythm in movement and dance.

So today, why not join the angels in praising God? They promised peace on earth among those whom he favours—which is us, those to whom he's sent his son. That has to be worth celebrating. So find a favourite hymn or worship song and sing it (if your voice is like mine find somewhere private so you're not inhibited), or put on a special CD, and let your body praise God in movement and dance.

The incarnation which we're celebrating at the Christmas season is all about God becoming flesh, so our flesh is blessed by God and meant to praise him.

In the beginning

Reflective

A new year makes most of us reflective, for good or ill. We look back on what has been, and we wonder what the new year will hold. We may look ahead with anticipation—to a birth, a wedding, a new start at work or study— or with dread—surgery or sickness, a loved one moving away, or simply the unknown.

Take some time to reflect on the new year with God by your side. You might like to read Genesis 1 and John 1:1–18 as a way of grounding your reflection in God and his work.

In the beginning... God created the heavens and the earth—everything that is has its origin in God, from the farthest stars in the universe to the tiniest creatures and plants. Set a picture of your own life within this bigger picture. Remember your favourite places and creatures and give thanks that God sustains them, and sustains you.

In the beginning... was the Word—Jesus came in flesh to share our vulnerable, beautiful, risky lives. If there is something you are worrying about in the new year, sit quietly and see yourself walking through it with Jesus walking alongside you. Talk to him about your anxieties and listen for any answers. Then give thanks to him for the gifts you anticipate or simply for his continued presence with you, whether you always feel it or not.

In the beginning... what would you like to begin for you in this new year? Is there something you need to let go of to enable this? Is there something you need to do to make this new thing a reality? What one resolution do you want to make? Ask for God's help in putting it into practice.

Listening to the word with Wycliffe

Story

One of the lesser known saints remembered in this season is John Wycliffe, whose day falls on 31 December.

He and his followers, the Lollards, were in many ways forerunners of the Reformation in England. Born in Yorkshire around 1330, he moved to Oxford to study and spent most of the rest of his life there, teaching and writing books. He campaigned against the privileged status of the clergy (despite being ordained himself), exalted the Bible as the ultimate authority in Christian life and supported the authority of the king against that of the pope in temporal matters. These positions frequently got him into trouble and he was summoned to Lambeth Palace to defend his teaching. In the 1380s a number of his teachings were declared to be heretical and others erroneous. He died at the very end of 1384.

Wycliffe's belief in the importance of the Bible led him to produce one of the first translations of the Bible into English; he himself probably translated the Gospels and perhaps the rest of the New Testament, with others undertaking the Old Testament. It was completed near the end of his life and revised soon afterwards by one of his associates. There are around 150 copies of the manuscript of this version, showing how widely it must have been circulated in England.

Remembering Wycliffe and other translators of the Bible brings home to us the importance of being able to read the Bible in our own language—something we may take for granted when books are so readily available. Perhaps as a way of showing your gratitude you might want to consider supporting a charity which translates the Bible into those languages which still do not have it.

It's also important for each of us to find ways of 'reading' God in a language which is meaningful—consider what 'language' you best use to think of and relate to God; not this time an actual language (English, French, Chinese)—but the languages of words, images, silence, metaphors or action. Which of these makes God most vivid to you and best enables you to respond? Perhaps your best language is something else again? Use this language to respond to the gift of God's word, both the written word and the Word made flesh. Use your language to tell you of its importance for you.

Called by name

Reflective

On New Year's Day the Church keeps the feast of the naming of Jesus, remembering how, eight days after his birth, his parents took him to be circumcised, in keeping with Jewish tradition, and to be given the name which the angel Gabriel had announced to Mary (Luke 2:21).

Our name matters—it links us to our family and our country

of origin if we're given a name which generations before us have had. It may reflect a passion of our parents if we have the name of their favourite musician, film star or footballer, or perhaps a desire to be unique if we're given a name no one else has. Jesus' name describes who he is—the Saviour, the one who brings God's salvation to the world. And this name was his from before his birth. Jeremiah the prophet went even further; he heard God saying to him, 'Before I formed you in the womb I knew you' (Jeremiah 1:5).

Our names matter—being called by name is a sign of friendship and of belonging. We instinctively know this; we feel embarrassed if we can't remember the name of someone who we should know or give them the wrong name.

One of the pleasures of religious life is the chance to choose a new or additional name when joining. In the past you were simply given a name (which may or may not have been a blessing); but now we are encouraged to keep our baptismal name and perhaps to add something. I added Julian to my baptismal name of Helen because Julian of Norwich had been important to me as I reflected on my possible vocation.

If you had the chance to choose a new or additional name, what would it be and why?

Stand before God with that name; allow him to use it to call you.

Reflect on God knowing you from before your birth and listen for God calling your name.

As a Child

Phil Steer

Belongs

*'Let the little children come to me, and do not hinder
them, for the kingdom of heaven belongs to such
as these'.*
MATTHEW 19:14, NIV 1984, EMPHASIS MINE

When I was younger my dad had a rather nice record deck.
Not unreasonably he wasn't keen on the idea of me and my
brothers using and abusing it, so it was strictly 'off limits'—at
least until we were older and had learnt how to treat it properly.
If we wanted to play our records, then we had our own (rather
cheaper) record player; or we could ask Dad if he would mind
putting our records on his deck.

Some people regard the kingdom of heaven in much the same
way. They think that the things of the kingdom are reserved for
those who are older, wiser and more mature in their faith. Some
even believe that the only way they can have access to God and
his kingdom is through the ministries of priests or elders or other
church leaders—rather in the same way that we children could
use Dad's record deck only by asking him to put the records
on for us. Even if this is not what we truly believe, we can still
find ourselves thinking and behaving as if this were the case—
hanging on to the coat-tails of 'famous' and 'successful' teachers
and healers and worship-leaders, as if it were only through their
ministries and ministrations that we truly expect to hear and
receive and encounter the living God.

But this is not what Jesus says. Rather, all of the riches and resources of the kingdom are freely available—without restriction or reservation—to all who come to God as little children; for the kingdom, we are told, 'belongs to such as these'.

But why should this be? Why should the kingdom belong to the childlike in particular?

First and foremost, these are the ones who feel most deeply that their true home is to be found in the kingdom of heaven. Of course, all believers are members of God's household (Ephesians 2:19), and find their home with him. Yet some of us behave more like adolescent teenagers, pushing boundaries and craving independence; or else like young adults, outwardly conforming to the 'house rules' yet inwardly hankering after a place of our own, where we are free to live how we choose. Little children are not like this. They know that their home is with their parents: this is where they belong, this is where they will find love and care and protection. And, in the same way, the childlike know that they belong in the kingdom, at home with their heavenly Father, and they have no desire to be anywhere else.

The kingdom of heaven belongs to the childlike just as our family home belongs to my children. It is not that they are the legal owners—indeed, I doubt very much they would welcome having to pay the mortgage! Rather, it belongs to them because, as our children and as a part of our family, they have the right to live here. Indeed, so much more than the right, which suggests some sense of grudging obligation; rather, as their mum and dad we delight to have them with us. They belong in the family home and, as such, the family home belongs to them.

In the same way, Jesus assures us, as God's children we belong in his Father's house—so much so that he himself has gone to prepare a place for us, that we might be with him where he is (John 14:2–3). Imagine that! Jesus, the King of kings and Lord of lords getting your room ready for you. And this place in his kingdom belongs to us by right—not because of anything that we have done to earn it or deserve it, but simply as adopted sons and daughters of God. As the apostle Paul wrote to the churches in Galatia, 'God sent his Son... that we might receive the full rights of sons' (Galatians 4:4–5).

Of course, we will fully inherit our heavenly home only when, at the last, we go to be with Jesus; and yet, it belongs to us here and now. The kingdom of heaven is our true home, the family home, our home as children of our heavenly Father. It is where we abide and where we rest, where we are fed and where we grow, where we know love and where we feel secure, the place from which we go out into the world and the place to which we return.

It is the Church, the fellowship of believers, the body of Christ. But it is so much more than this. It is wherever God finds a welcome in the world and wherever he finds a welcome in our lives. As we make our home with God in his kingdom, so he makes his home with us (John 14:23) and forms his kingdom within us (Luke 17:21). This is the measure of what he has given; this is how much the kingdom belongs to us: it becomes a very part of us. We belong in God's kingdom and his kingdom belongs in us.

But not only does God give the childlike a home in his kingdom, he gives them all of its riches and resources also. As Paul wrote to the church in Rome, '[God] did not spare his own Son, but gave him up for us all—how will he not also, along with him, graciously give us all things?' (Romans 8:32). There are no age restrictions, nothing is out of bounds—the childlike can have it all.

But can this really be the case? Would God really give the things of the kingdom to those who will treat them like little children? After all, as parents it would be irresponsible of us to allow our children to play with anything and everything within our home. There are things that we must keep from them, both for their own protection and to keep our possessions safe from harm.

Because let's be realistic about this: little children tend not to be very good at looking after the things they are given. They bash them and drop them and throw them around, and try to use them in ways for which they were never designed. Their toys get broken, their books get bent, their clothes get torn. They have little or no idea of the value of what they have, and rarely look after their possessions as they should. Does Jesus really mean that the kingdom of God belongs to such as these? Surely they can't be trusted and entrusted with something of such worth?

Now without doubt, as the perfect parent, God does at times withhold things from us until we are truly ready to receive them and use them properly. Yet many a time he is far more willing to give to those who have a childlike approach than to those who are more grown up in their handling of what they've been given.

Like many young boys, as a child I had quite a collection of die-cast model vehicles. I raced them across the room, crashed them into walls and each other, even flew them through the air; then I scooped them up and dropped them together in a drawer, or left them scattered across the floor, waiting to be crushed beneath someone's feet. Inevitably, after a while they became rather the worse for wear: the paintwork got chipped, the windows got scratched, the wheels got bent.

Today these same toys are marketed and sold as 'collectibles', and early models in pristine condition can be worth a small fortune—especially if they are still in their original packaging. 'If only I'd been more careful!' I might think. Adult collectors would never dream of treating these models with the same casual disregard that I did as a child. They are properly looked after and protected from damage. Displayed in cabinets like ornaments or even shut up in boxes and stored safely away, there's no chance of them ending up in the same state as my childhood toys. And yet it seems wrong, somehow, for any toy to be treated like this: never having been played with by a child, never having fired his imagination, never having elicited her affection, never having brought a youngster pleasure and joy, never having fulfilled the purpose for which it was created.

Jesus tells a famous story of a man who went on a journey, entrusting money to his three servants (Matthew 25:14–30). Two of the servants used what they'd been given to make more money for their master, and were commended for their efforts. The third, however, hid the money in the ground, returning it with the words, 'I was afraid… See here is what belongs to you.' Hearing the tale for the first time we might reasonably expect that this servant would receive at least some credit for keeping his master's money safe and returning it intact. But not a bit of it. Instead, he receives nothing but condemnation. Why? Because he has made no use of what he's been given.

It is all too easy for us to fall into behaving like this third servant, so fearful of failure and loss that we fail to use the gifts that we've been given. We are only too well aware of the value of what we have, and of how fragile and fleeting it can be. This applies not only to our physical possessions, but perhaps more especially to those far more precious things: our family and friends, our health and happiness, our time and activities, our hopes and dreams—all that life entails, and ultimately life itself.

And so we play it safe. We look to protect what we have. Preservation becomes our first priority. Rather than using all we've been given, we bury it in the ground.

We might not admit it—perhaps even to ourselves—but as Christians we can be especially fearful of losing the very thing that makes us what we are—our faith in Christ. We fear that we may be tested and found wanting, that we may be seduced by the undoubted attractions of the world, that our faith may crumble and fall if we allow our foundation of simple certainties to be undermined. And so we shy away from encountering the world as it really is—with all its complexities and contradictions, its certainties and doubts, its sorrows and joys. We shut ourselves up in a box—in our godly ghetto, our holy huddle—to keep ourselves safe and secure. Just witness the siege mentality that the church so often adopts when it feels threatened by the world.

But, paradoxically, in seeking to protect and preserve our life and faith in this way, we can end up losing the very thing that we are trying to keep. Like the servant in the parable, if we do not use what has been entrusted to us, it will be taken from us. As Jesus warns us, 'Whoever wants to save his life will lose it, but whoever loses his life for me will save it' (Luke 9:24).

And so, we need to be like little children: not keeping the myriad gifts that we've been given shut up 'safely' in their boxes, but delighting to use them all with childlike abandon—for 'the kingdom of heaven belongs to such as these'.

Spotlight:
Desert retreats

Fay Cox

For centuries deserts have offered sanctuary to those seeking a place of refuge or retreat. Their stark beauty and isolation strip everything back to the bare necessities of daily living, creating the space and time for quiet reflection. Many say that this is where silence can be found in its purest form—an increasingly rare commodity in our modern world.

The desert of South Sinai offers a unique and inspiring venue for a retreat, with its dramatic scenery and many biblical associations. This is where Moses led the Israelites, saw the burning bush and received the ten commandments; where Elijah heard the 'still, small voice' and knew that it was the presence of God. South Sinai became a home for reclusive and ascetic fourth-century Christian desert fathers and mothers, who lived in solitary caves or small communities, away from civilisation, in order to practise their faith without distraction. These early monastics experienced a life of hardship and relative solitude that gave them deep insights into human spiritual nature which have been passed down through oral tradition. The Orthodox Monastery of St Catherine was also established here, built at the foot of Mount Sinai, where continuous Christian worship has been offered daily since the sixth century, possibly longer than anywhere else in the world.

Continuing this long tradition of pilgrimage and retreat, Wind Sand & Stars is a specialist tour company that offers high-quality historical and spiritual journeys. Our story began nearly 25 years ago when, in discovering the beauty and many treasures of

South Sinai, we forged close friendships with the local Bedouin. The families of the Muzeina tribe welcomed us to their desert homes and have become an integral part of our authentic and intimate desert journeys, always offering us their hospitality as they share their traditional way of life with us.

'I am hugely impressed with Wind Sand & Stars organisation and their relationship with the Bedouin family who looked after us. These local contacts made the experience especially rich. The simplicity of our living conditions allowed the desert to come alive and enrich the search for silence' (a traveller with Wind Sand & Stars).

Our retreats are based in a remote and beautiful part of South Sinai in a traditional Bedouin-style camp. Days will normally involve a rhythm of worship and prayer, with periods alone in silence, as well as optional excursions on foot and camel.

All meals are freshly prepared over a camp fire. In the evening there is time to relax together around the fire, sharing the events of the day and enjoying the remarkable desert night skies with cups of hot, sweet Bedouin tea, before sleeping out under the stars each night.

Some journeys may involve travel through desert valleys, following ancient pilgrimage routes towards St Catherine's Monastery and Mount Sinai, moving at the gentle pace of traditional desert travel and experiencing Bedouin life at first hand—riding on camels, taking in the desert valleys and canyons, over hills and sand dunes, past scattered oases, the views changing constantly.

For many, a highlight is the chance to visit St Catherine's Monastery, with its magnificent Basilica and rare collections of early Christian icons and manuscripts. An ascent of Mount Sinai, a stiff two to three hours' walk, is rewarded by breathtaking views from the summit of the surrounding desert and mountains. Accommodation can also be arranged at the Monastery guesthouse.

Our guest speakers will guide and inspire the group along the way, sharing their knowledge and giving insights into this ancient landscape and its remarkable tales. They include members of the clergy, academics and specialists, including the writer Sara Maitland who leads the annual non-denominational *Adventure into Silence*.

'This was an extraordinary experience: As much silence as you could wish for on a trip of this type; opportunities to balance the silence with a carefully and thoughtfully planned programme; the Bedouin hospitality and culture. I would seriously consider this becoming part of my retreat programme every year, it is so rich and rewarding and nourishing. Thank you' (a traveller with Wind Sand & Stars).

Wind Sand & Stars is experienced in helping those who have never ventured into this type of environment before, as well as offering unusual opportunities for those seeking new retreat experiences. Tailor-made journeys can also be arranged for individuals and groups, from overnight excursions to 40 days in the desert.

Details of all of our historical and spiritual journeys can be found on our website www.windsandstars.co.uk, including historical tours to Ethiopia and Armenia.

Contact 01256 886543 option 7 or email office@windsandstars.co.uk.

Using *Quiet Spaces* with a group

As we approach Christmas, groups often want something reflective for the season; a way of entering the true Christmas spirit. If you are asked this year you could try using some of the *Quiet Spaces* material. Here is a suggestion of what you might do based on the Gifts section.

You will need:
A selection of wrapping paper, ribbon, sticky tape
Small boxes (empty packaging)
Gift tags or shiny card for people to use to make tags
Pens
Scissors

Open with a prayer:

Lord, as we meet together, may we also each meet with you and be open and ready to hear your voice. As we get ready for Christmas, a time of giving and receiving, help us now to be ready to receive from you, from your abundant gifts.

Invite the group to choose a box and to wrap it up carefully, as a precious gift. This is going to be a gift to someone else in the room, a gift from God. Encourage them to do this silently, concentrating on doing the best they can with their wrapping, and they can acknowledge God with them as they wrap his present from him. Ask them to put a gift tag on their parcel, but to leave the tag empty.

When all the parcels are wrapped and the mess has been cleared away, stack the presents in the middle of the room.

Invite each person to take a box and to receive it as a gift from God. Ask them to hold their parcel, to receive it, to acknowledge to God the gift they are holding.

As they hold the gift, they listen to God. What does he want to say to them? What does he want to put on the gift tag? When they are ready they can write on the tag what God wants to say to them.

You could then use either the section called, 'What I can I give him' or 'Christ as gift'. You can read the section aloud, pausing to give the group time to enter the scene, or think.

Then allow some quiet time for their conversations with Jesus, or sit with Mary as she ponders who her baby will be.

When it seems that most people are ready to move on, invite them to get into pairs and to share as much, or as little, of what they have experienced as they would like.

They can then take their presents home as a reminder of God's gifts to them.

BRF Quiet Days

BRF Quiet Days are an ideal way of redressing the balance in our busy lives. Held in peaceful locations around the country, each one is led by an experienced speaker and gives the opportunity to reflect, be silent and pray, and through it all to draw closer to God.

Wednesday 28 September: 'Between a Rock and a Hard Place' led by Debbie Thrower at Old Alresford Place, Alresford, Hampshire SO24 9DH

Friday 14 October: 'Exploring Creative Prayer Ideas' led by Claire Daniel at Shallowford House, Stone, Staffordshire ST15 0NZ

Wednesday 19 October: 'Let the Trees Clap Their Hands' led by Margot and Martin Hodson at Carmelite Priory, Boars Hill, Oxford OX1 5HB

Wednesday 16 November: 'Timing Out in Advent' led by Gordon Giles at House of Retreat, The Street, Pleshey, Chelmsford, CM3 1HA

For further details and to book, please go to www.brfonline.org.uk/events-and-quiet-days or contact us at BRF, 15 The Chambers, Vineyard, Abingdon, Oxfordshire OX14 3FE; tel: 01865 319700.

Lighted Windows

An Advent calendar for a world in waiting

Margaret Silf

From bestselling author Margaret Silf, this brand-new edition of *Lighted Windows* offers readings, reflections, prayers or points for meditation for every single day from 1 December to 6 January (Epiphany), based around the main theme of looking through the 'windows' of human experience and discovering more about God, and his call to men and women to follow him. It is also a testimony to the power of waiting—as people wait for Christmas through the Advent season, and as the birth of the Messiah was awaited through the centuries. Waiting can be difficult at times—but Christmas proves the value of patience, and of taking time to stop, to look out, to listen.

ISBN 978 0 85746 432 3   £7.99
Available from your local Christian bookshop or direct from BRF: visit www.brfonline.org.uk

Also available for Kindle: see www.brfonline.org.uk/ebooks

Available from September 2016

Heaven's Morning

Rethinking the destination

David Winter

The Bible—especially the New Testament—has plenty to say about resurrection and heaven, but many Christians struggle to make sense of what it actually means in practice. David Winter's accessible book explores the biblical teaching on what happens after death and considers what difference this can make to our lives here and now. He also shows how we can present what we believe about eternity as a source of hope to our sceptical, anxious world.

ISBN 978 0 85746 476 7   £7.99
Available from your local Christian bookshop or direct from BRF: visit www.brfonline.org.uk

Also available for Kindle: see www.brfonline.org.uk/ebooks

Confidence in the Living God

David & Goliath revisited

Andrew Watson

Confidence lies at the heart of society. As Christians, we are called to proclaim our faith in God, but how can we build and maintain this confidence in an increasingly secularised culture where such faith is often seen as marginal, embarrassing or even downright dangerous?

Using the story of David and Goliath as his starting point, Andrew Watson shows how the Lord can indeed be our confidence, whatever the odds. He explores how God can develop a proper self-confidence within individuals and his Church, revealing the gospel through transforming words and transformed lives. He considers, too, how we can confidently tackle the challenges of day-to-day living, whether a difficult work situation or family relationship, or simply anxiety about the future. The book includes a discussion guide and is ideal as a whole church course on the subject of confidence.

ISBN 978 0 85746 482 8   £7.99
Available from your local Christian bookshop or direct from BRF: visit www.brfonline.org.uk

Also available for Kindle: see www.brfonline.org.uk/ebooks

Believe in Miracles

A spiritual journey of positive change

Carmel Thomason

This book takes you on a 40-day journey into a world of possibility. Focusing on small practical steps, it offers a series of short exercises to promote lasting changes, leading to a more prayerful, contented and connected life. By looking for the good and focusing on actions to take now, you will learn to view differently your daily circumstances, your relationship with God, and your relationships with others, bringing something of the ways of heaven to earth.

ISBN 978 0 85746 420 0   £8.99
Available from your local Christian bookshop or direct from BRF: visit www.brfonline.org.uk

Also available for Kindle: see www.brfonline.org.uk/ebooks

QUIET SPACES SUBSCRIPTION FORM

All our Bible reading notes can be ordered online by visiting
www.biblereadingnotes.org.uk/subscriptions

If **you** and a minimum of **four** friends subscribe to *Quiet Spaces* or BRF's other Bible reading notes (*New Daylight, Day by Day with God, Guidelines, The Upper Room*), you can form a group. What's so good about being in a group? You pay the price of the notes only —postage is free for delivery to a UK address. (All notes are sent to one address.) All group orders are invoiced. No advance payment is required. For more information, see **www.biblereadingnotes.org.uk/group-subscriptions/** or contact the BRF office.

Title _____ First name/initials _____ Surname _____

Address _____

_____ Postcode _____

Telephone _____ Email _____

INDIVIDUAL SUBSCRIPTION Please send **Quiet Spaces** beginning with the January 2017 / May 2017 / September 2017 issue (*delete as appropriate*):

	Quantity	UK	Europe	Rest of World
(per 3 issues)	☐	☐ £16.35	☐ £24.45	☐ £28.20

Total enclosed £ _____ (*cheques should be made payable to 'BRF'*)

Please charge my Mastercard ☐ Visa ☐ Debit card ☐ with £ _____

Card no. ☐☐☐☐ ☐☐☐☐ ☐☐☐☐ ☐☐☐☐

Valid from [M][M][Y][Y]   Expires [M][M][Y][Y]

Security code* ☐☐☐   *Last 3 digits on the reverse of the card
ESSENTIAL IN ORDER TO PROCESS YOUR ORDER

Signature _____ Date ___ / ___ / ___
(*essential if paying by credit card*)

To set up a Direct Debit, please also complete the Direct Debit instruction on the reverse of this form.

GROUP SUBSCRIPTION (UK only) Please send **Quiet Spaces** beginning with the January 2017 / May 2017 / September 2017 issue (*delete as appropriate*):

Quantity ☐ (Current price per issue: £4.35)

Please invoice me: per issue / annually (*delete as appropriate*).

---

*To read our terms and find out about cancelling your order,
please visit www.brfonline.org.uk/terms*

Please return, with appropriate payment as necessary, to:
BRF, 15 The Chambers, Vineyard, Abingdon OX14 3FE

QS0316 The Bible Reading Fellowship (BRF) is a Registered Charity (233280). VAT No: GB 238 5574 35

The Bible Reading Fellowship

Instruction to your bank or building society to pay by Direct Debit

Please fill in the whole form using a ballpoint pen and return it to:
BRF, 15 The Chambers, Vineyard, Abingdon OX14 3FE

Service User Number:

5	5	8	2	2	9

Name and full postal address of your bank or building society

To: The Manager	Bank/Building Society
Address	
	Postcode

Name(s) of account holder(s)

Branch sort code	**Bank/Building Society account number**

Reference

Instruction to your Bank/Building Society
Please pay The Bible Reading Fellowship Direct Debits from the account detailed in this instruction, subject to the safeguards assured by the Direct Debit Guarantee. I understand that this instruction may remain with The Bible Reading Fellowship and, if so, details will be passed electronically to my bank/building society.

Signature(s)

Banks and Building Societies may not accept Direct Debit instructions for some types of account.

QS0316

DIRECT DEBIT PAYMENT

You can pay for your annual subscription to our Bible reading notes using Direct Debit. You need only give your bank details once, and the payment is made automatically every year until you cancel it. If you would like to pay by Direct Debit, please use the form opposite, entering your BRF account number under 'Reference'.

You are fully covered by the Direct Debit Guarantee:

The Direct Debit Guarantee

· This Guarantee is offered by all banks and building societies that accept instructions to pay Direct Debits.

· If there are any changes to the amount, date or frequency of your Direct Debit, The Bible Reading Fellowship will notify you 10 working days in advance of your account being debited or as otherwise agreed. If you request The Bible Reading Fellowship to collect a payment, confirmation of the amount and date will be given to you at the time of the request.

· If an error is made in the payment of your Direct Debit, by The Bible Reading Fellowship or your bank or building society, you are entitled to a full and immediate refund of the amount paid from your bank or building society.

· If you receive a refund you are not entitled to, you must pay it back when The Bible Reading Fellowship asks you to.

· You can cancel a Direct Debit at any time by simply contacting your bank or building society. Written confirmation may be required. Please also notify us.

This page is for your notes.